Jonjo Mauds

T0270195

111 Places
in Windsor
That You
Shouldn't Miss

Photographs by James Riley

emons:

© Emons Verlag GmbH
All rights reserved
© Photographs by James Riley, except:
ch. 71: Royal Collection Trust / © His Majesty King Charles III 2023
© Cover icon: Shutterstock.com/Daniel De Petro
Layout: Eva Kraskes, based on a design
by Lübbeke | Naumann | Thoben
Maps: altancicek.design, www.altancicek.de
Basic cartographical information from Openstreetmap,
© OpenStreetMap-Mitwirkende, OdbL
Edited by: Ros Horton
Printing and binding: Grafisches Centrum Cuno, Calbe
Printed in Germany 2023
ISBN 978-3-7408-2009-1
First edition

Guidebooks for Locals & Experienced Travellers
Join us in uncovering new places around the world at
www.111places.com

Foreword

If you're looking for a guidebook to Windsor Castle, you won't find it here. Nor will you find Legoland, the Long Walk, or any of Windsor's other tourist traps. If this is your first time in Windsor, we're sure you'll discover these places easily enough on your own. What you'll instead find in this book is a celebration of Windsor off the beaten track, told through various lenses: local history, urban myths, and the stories of people who have, and still are helping this town to break out of the shadow of the castle, and emerge as a destination in its own right.

In writing this book, we have travelled to places that have played a vital role in shaping the town's identity. What you will come to discover is that Windsor is not just the home of the royal family – it's home of tens of thousands of interesting, innovative and inspiring commoners, too. From craft beer breweries reviving Windsor's brewing heritage, to artists who are filling the town with intrigue and wonder, to patches of earth bursting with hidden history, and of course the local legends that add meaning to otherwise inconspicuous things. We couldn't resist venturing into those aforementioned tourist traps a few times, but what we've returned with are stories that transcend the ordinary.

We'll take you around Windsor as two locals would. We'll point you to places other guidebooks wouldn't dare venture. We'll regale you with fascinating stories of places hidden in plain sight. We'll show you how art, architecture and even infrastructure have played their part. And we'll break out of Windsor to see how the town fits into its wider borough, and the influence it has had on other nearby towns. Ultimately, we leave you with a book that celebrates the places – and the people – that make Windsor a cool, quirky and truly unique place.

111 Places

1 4 Privet Drive

A perfectly normal house, thank you very much

On 1 November, 1989, a mysterious wizard named Dumbledore appeared outside this quiet suburban abode. With his magical cigarette lighter, he extracted the light from all the streetlamps down the road. Moments later, he was joined by a transforming witch by the name of Professor McGonagall, and the half-giant Hagrid, who arrived on a flying motorbike clutching a baby boy. The mysterious trio placed the boy on the doorstep along with a letter, made out to Mr and Mrs Dursley of 4 Privet Drive, Little Whinging, Surrey. That boy would grow up to be none other than Harry Potter, the 'Boy Who Lived'.

And it all happened right here. In 2000, this street in Martins Heron was transformed into the dreary neighbourhood of Privet Drive for *Harry Potter and the Philosopher's Stone* (or *Sorcerer's Stone* to you Americans), the first instalment in a film franchise that would go on to be the fifth highest-grossing of all time. The house at 12 Picket Post Close played the starring role of 4 Privet Drive, where Daniel Radcliffe lived as Harry Potter in the cupboard under the stairs. It was here that he received his invitation to Hogwarts from Hedwig, played by Ook the owl, by way of an avalanche of letters bursting out of the fireplace (all done with live practical effects).

For the disruption they'd endured, the residents of Picket Post Close were offered a small fee, but when they tried to up their rates for the second film, the producers decided it would be cheaper to build their own Privet Drive at Leavesden Studios. Today, a replica of 12 Picket Post Close can be seen as part of the Warner Bros. Studio Tour in Watford, and there's even a Lego model of the home. Almost setting the record for the most expensive piece of Harry Potter memorabilia, the house sold in 2018 for the sum of £435,000. The new owners are accommodating of fans, but do be mindful to respect their privacy.

Address 12 Picket Post Close, Martins Heron, Bracknell RG12 9FG | Getting there Train to Martins Heron | Hours Private house, but can be viewed from the outside | Tip Fans of Terry Gilliam's 1981 smash hit *Time Bandits* may also like to visit Haywood (RG12 7WG), which was the home of the film's protagonist, Kevin.

2 — 21 Arthur Road

Crime, punishment, and the poem it inspired

'Each man kills the thing they love.' On the night of 29 March, 1896, one man did exactly that.

Charles Wooldridge was a trooper in the Royal Horse Guards who spent several years at Windsor. There he met and subsequently married Nell Glendell, the love of his life. Not long after, his regiment moved to London, but Nell was unable to move with her husband. The long distance put a strain on their marriage, and on the few occasions they got to see each other, fiery arguments would break out.

The marriage started to break down after Wooldridge assaulted poor Nell, after which she reverted to her maiden name and possibly started an affair. Furious, Charles travelled back to Windsor with a cut-throat razor in his pocket. At Nell's home on Alma Terrace, 21 Arthur Road, a fight erupted, eventually spilling onto the street outside. There, Charles took his razor and slashed his wife's throat. When the police arrived, he made no attempt to flee or resist. 'Take me!' he cried in front of a crowd of onlookers. 'I have killed my wife!' At the subsequent trial, the jury took just two minutes to decide that the murder was premeditated and therefore worthy of the maximum sentence, which, in those days, was death by hanging.

For six weeks the guardsman walked the yard at Reading Gaol, all the while showing immense remorse for his crime. Then, on the morning of 7 July, it was time for him to swing. One man who stood in the crowd beneath the gallows that day was the Irish poet Oscar Wilde, incarcerated for two years on the charge of gross indecency. The scene of Wooldridge's execution had a profound effect on Wilde, inspiring one of his seminal works, *The Ballad of Reading Gaol*. As much a recount of Wooldridge's bitter end, it is a treatise on life and death and all the sadness in between. 'The man had killed the thing he loved,' wrote Wilde. 'And so he had to die.'

Address 21 Arthur Road, Windsor SL4 1RS | **Getting there** Train to either Windsor & Eton Central or Windsor & Eton Riverside; bus 2, 8, 702 or 703 | **Hours** Private house, but can be viewed from the outside | **Tip** In the adjacent Ward Royal estate you'll find The Hope, a community-run pub that, depending on the day, may also double as a live music venue or flea market.

3___A329

Take me home, turnpike road

Getting to Windsor nowadays couldn't be easier. As well as two train stations, the town has its own exit on the M4 and many roads in from the south – the B3022 bowls past Legoland, the A322 trundles through Windsor Great Park, and the A308 links up with the M25 via Runnymede and Old Windsor.

Suffice to say it wasn't always so simple. Getting to Windsor was once only feasible by river boat, unless you felt like pushing your carriage through miles of mud along some centuries-old forest footpath. The coming of Windsor's first legitimate highway was a bit of a revolution, and is contained in the wider story of England's 'Turnpike Road' system. The Windsor Forest Turnpike, inaugurated in 1759, still follows roughly the same route today in the guise of the A329: from Reading, it travels through Wokingham, Bracknell and Ascot before terminating in the leafy south-east corner of the Great Park.

While today it is a busy urban thoroughfare, this turnpike started life as a humble dirt road. Funds for its upkeep were collected from toll gates, with one ox charged at the same rate as two horses, and fares running twice as high in the sludgy winter months, when vehicles left deeper ruts in the road surface. While the building itself may be long gone, one such toll gate is remembered in the name 'Blacknest Gate', now the southernmost entrance to the Great Park.

The responsibility for maintaining the Windsor Forest Turnpike fell to influential men representing the different villages of the Great Forest, who met annually at The Rose in Wokingham to discuss and distribute their revenue. The labourers they employed were paid in beer, which was given in stronger and more abundant supply as the years went by. How's that for an inflation-busting pay rise? Mind you, that might also explain why the road was, apparently, always found in a fairly shoddy state…

Tip While travelling along the A329 through Bracknell, look out for the road 'Old Tollgate Close' (RG12 9RQ), named as such by local history group The Bracknell Forest Society, who believe the cottage at the end to be part of the original toll gate.

4　Abandoned Part of the M4
Road to nowhere

Maidenhead is the birthplace of the M4, the section between Junction 7 and Thicket Roundabout being the first to be officially opened in 1962. But hang on, you say, the M4 doesn't go to Thicket Roundabout! Well oh boy, strap in, because we're about to take a high-octane drive through motorway history.

In the early days, the M4 took a slightly different route, terminating at Maidenhead Thicket where it linked up with the A4. The original plan was to extend it westwards from here, going north of Reading and on to the West Country. Unfortunately, this would have taken the motorway through picturesque villages like Twyford and Sonning – suffice to say, this idea was not popular with local residents.

Thus, the route was redirected, the new course going south of Reading. In order to achieve this, a number of changes needed to be made at the section around Maidenhead: first came the Holyport Interchange, opened in 1971, which marked the start of the extension; Junction 8, deemed too close to the new interchange, was subsequently closed (parts of it can still be seen today – a depot on Priors Way is built on one of the old slip roads), while Holyport Interchange took on the unique designation of 'Junction 8/9'; the section of the M4 to Thicket Roundabout was then rebranded the A404 (M), while a new bypass, and possibly England's shortest motorway – the A308 (M) – was built to make up for the loss of Junction 8.

One casualty in all of this was a tract of road that would have linked the M4 with the A404 (M). The scars of this abandoned piece of infrastructure can be seen as you look to your left driving down the A308 (M), but the easiest (and safest) place to spot them is *Google Earth* – look for the unnaturally smooth curve through a copse of trees just north of the interchange. Look really close, and you may even spot chunks of asphalt the engineers left behind.

Address Holyport Interchange, Maidenhead | Getting there Junction 8/9 on the M4 | Tip Drive the route of the old M4 (now the A404 (M)) up to Maidenhead Thicket, where a beautiful nature trail around the ruins of a Celtic farmstead awaits you.

5 Air Forces Memorial

A monument on the edge of heaven

After climbing the spiral stairs to the top of the tower, you are greeted by a simply staggering view. On a clear day, the whole of London can be made out in the distance, from the swooping arch of Wembley Stadium to the jagged cluster of skyscrapers in the City. To the north-west, Windsor Castle looks like Stonehenge on the horizon. Below you is Runnymede, the birthplace of democracy which many have fought and died for. From this vantage point, you can follow the path of planes making their descent into Heathrow.

There is an old saying among pilots that goes: 'Any landing you can walk away from is a good landing.' The landings into Heathrow always seem to be good. Sadly, in the theatre of war, there are many of what – by that standard – we would have to call bad landings. The names of 20,000 airmen and women who were victims of such events are commemorated here, in a memorial perched so high on the peak of Cooper's Hill we might call it a cenotaph in the clouds.

Architecturally, the memorial is astonishing. Designed by Sir Edward Maufe (better known for Guildford Cathedral) and unveiled in 1953, it takes the form of a flight control tower built of white stone, the centre of which can be climbed to discover the aforementioned view. This central monolith is surrounded by a cloistered quadrangle, with two wings spreading out across the hillside. Upon every wall are the names of the fallen – a masterful use of glass ensures that the dedications are always illuminated by the light of the Sun. The ceilings are decorated with the coats of arms of former dominions of the British Empire, painted by Maufe's long-term collaborator John Hutton.

In the distance, the world moves at a frantic pace, but here it is as if time is frozen. Sit, rest, reflect. Enjoy the tranquillity and isolation, and give thanks to those who tragically never came back down to Earth.

Address Cooper's Hill Lane, Englefield Green TW20 0LB | Getting there Train to Egham, then a 30-minute walk; bus 1, 8 or 440 to Cooper's Hill Lane | Hours Feb–Oct Mon–Fri 8.30am–6pm, Sat & Sun 10am–6pm; Nov–Jan Mon–Fri 8.30am–4pm, Sat & Sun 10am–4pm | Tip For a change of pace, walk to the bottom of Cooper's Hill Lane to discover Maranello, one of the UK's premier dealerships for Maserati and Ferrari supercars, housed in a stunning 1935 Art Deco building.

6 Ankerwycke Yew

The silent witness to Magna Carta

Historians have long debated the exact location where Magna Carta was signed. The best contender is Magna Carta Island (named after the fact), an ait on the north bank of the Thames. It is a low-lying, clay-smothered island, populated mainly by grazing cattle and an array of trees: oak, pine, chestnut, all wrapped up in luscious green ivy.

The most significant of these trees is Ankerwycke Yew, which is ancient enough to have seen the signing of Magna Carta itself. In fact, it is thought to be even older than that – its proprietors, the National Trust, believe it to be around 2,500 years old.

Getting to this behemoth is a challenge that will require wellies. But your reward for trudging through the muddy fields comes when you suddenly find yourself beneath a row of silver birch trees leading to a meadow full of snowdrops, where, in their midst, you'll spot the mighty Yew. Age has wrinkled and warped this great beast – its trunk has cleft itself apart several times, only to regenerate by plunging arterial branches back into the soil – but the rich swatches of red across its bark tell us that it has plenty of life left in it yet.

Just opposite are the ruins of Ankerwycke Priory, a short-lived Benedictine nunnery dating from the 12th century until the Reformation. The state you see it in today is not all that dissimilar to how it would have looked in its heyday. It was apparently so dilapidated, its living conditions so horrid, that many of its sisters escaped into the nearby town of Wraysbury to bunk with the local men.

Be sure to finish your journey by walking the trail around the perimeter of the island. Look out for the statue of Queen Elizabeth II, sculpted by James Butler and raised in 2015 to honour the 800th year of Magna Carta. From across the river, the late Queen gazes appreciatively at the site where the course of English history was changed for ever.

Address Magna Carta Lane, Wraysbury TW19 5AF, www.nationaltrust.org.uk/visit/surrey/runnymede-and-ankerwycke | **Getting there** Bus 305 to Magna Carta Lane; by road, do not trust your satnav – it might plonk you on the wrong side of the river. Instead, set your destination to Magna Carta Lane via the B376. There is a small National Trust car park at the start of the trail. | **Tip** Mancunians will find a familiar yet peculiar sight in the back garden of Ivy Cottage at the end of the trail. The owner appears to have procured a beaten-up Magic Bus, one of the city's popular Stagecoach buses.

7___Ascot Locomotive Society
The Racecourse line

You won't find Royal Ascot Station on any railway maps, which is odd considering how busy it gets. Trains from all over the world converge on this spot, with trainspotters and young children alike struggling to contain their excitement at the sight of the Union Pacific Big Boy, or the Chesapeake & Ohio ALCO S-1. Then again, the station is not part of any railway network – its 820 yards of track form only a simple pleasure loop affording breathtaking views of Royal Ascot Golf Club and its centuries-old cherry trees, with a short whistle stop at Ascot United Football Club.

If you couldn't tell already, this is not a real station; rather, it is the headquarters of Ascot Locomotive Society, a community-run model railway. First formed in 1988, the scale railway has changed its course several times over the years as the interests of its next door neighbour, Ascot Racecourse, have demanded. But this has not stopped its members being there, week-in, week-out. The labour force is dwindling as many of them approach old age, but their driving ethos – to keep young people fascinated and inspired by engineering – keeps them coming back.

One member you're likely to bump into is former Chief Engineer Ian Rough. If you're lucky, Ian might let you ride his pride and joy: a royal blue Class 7, the only one of its kind in England, which he designed in honour of his French penpal Dominique. He'll also point you to some of his handiwork around the diorama – in particular, the enormous central turntable, which has become a popular way to end a journey.

If you start to feel a bit trainsick (who could blame you? Some of these locomotives get up to a top speed of 25 mph), stop by the break room for a complimentary cup of tea. Just remember to leave a donation while you're here, remembering the whole society is funded by the generosity of rail enthusiasts like you.

Address Winkfield Road, Ascot SL5 7LJ, ascotloco@hotmail.com | Getting there By car, follow Winkfield Road (A330) to the sign for 'Locomotive Society'. Follow the road past the golf club. The Locomotive Society is on the left, with free parking in the field opposite. | Hours Society meets first Sunday of each month from 2pm; open days May–Oct first Sunday of the month (weather permitting), 2–5.30pm | Tip At the High Street end of Winkfield Road is the newly opened Hedone Ascot, a boutique food and wine store, with a bakery and a butcher's that, between them, could give Harrods a run for its money.

8 Ascot Racecourse

A right royal day at the races

For one week in June, Ascot erupts with colour as dandies, dames and the royals themselves descend upon the town for the world-famous Royal Ascot Week. For men, the prescribed style is morning suits and top hats, while women have more creative licence, which they put to full effect – especially when it comes to the customary headwear. The hats on display range from glamorous to gaudy to grotesque, all of which make ample pickings for tabloid photographers. The competition to make it into the local newspapers' obligatory Ascot Week centrefolds gets particularly heated on the Thursday, known colloquially as Ladies' Day.

All of which says nothing of the main event: the horse racing. As one of the biggest race meetings in the world, Ascot is serious business for breeders, jockeys and gamblers alike. One of the most popular events is the opening race, the Queen Anne Stakes, which bears the name of the monarch whose vision transformed the bristly, barren Ascot Heath into what is today Britain's most expensive racecourse. The first race at Ascot took place on 11 August, 1711, for the grand prize of £50; today, the prize pot is more than £9 million.

Ascot's early years were turbulent, its reputation marred by pickpocketing and cockfighting, but when the flamboyant George IV spotted an opportunity to turn the event into his own miniature fashion parade, he gave us the Ascot we know and love today. The late Queen Elizabeth II was a huge patron of both the racing and the fashion – not only did she win the Gold Cup in 2013 with her horse Estimate, she also became the subject of Ascot's most popular flutter, which was to bet on the colour the queen would wear on a given day.

As for the other 51 weeks of the year, beer festivals, art fairs and fireworks events keep the racecourse busy, while during the day the landscaped heath is free to walk around.

Address High Street, Ascot SL5 7JX, +44 (0)344 3463611, www.ascot.com | Getting there Train to Ascot; bus 1, 24, 26 or 27 to Station Hill | Hours For events and opening times, see the website. Ascot Heath open daily on non-race days, 6.30am–7.30pm | Tip Haughty racegoers will invariably start their day with a posh brunch at Fego. But locals know the best way to fuel up for a day at the races is with a proper bacon butty in a crusty roll from Anne-Marie Patisserie (41A High Street).

9 __ Athens

Swimming in history

Start with your hands directly in front of you, thumbs touching, fingers together. Turn your knees outwards and kick your legs high and wide. Tuck in your toes and strike the soles of your feet against the water with each kick. Now move your arms backwards, dropping your elbows when they are level with your shoulders. Propel your arms forward, then pause for a second while continuing to kick. Congratulations! You've just learned to swim in John Leahy's 'Eton style'.

Leahy, one of Eton College's watermen, was a great contributor to the pedagogy of swimming. So committed was he to teaching, he not only wrote the book on it (*The Art of Swimming in the Eton Style*, published 1875), he also offered the poor children of Windsor discounted swimming lessons at the rate of one guinea. He even encouraged girls to learn, since it would make it easier for men to rescue them if they fell off their boats.

While today it is littered with 'No Swimming' signs, this stretch of the river was once the College's swimming bath, and Leahy's stomping ground. An illustration from his book shows how the College's watermen ran their lessons at Athens, with students suspended in the water from makeshift slings.

Historically owned by the Crown, Athens was bought for the College in 1917 by Hiatt Baker (whom University of Bristol alumni will surely recognise) in memory of his son John, who died in a flying accident. A stone by the bench commemorates Baker's gift, while on the other side is a comical extract from the College's 'Rules of the River', telling boys to hide their modesty should a lady come sailing past.

The classical (if slightly pretentious) name 'Athens' lives on in Eton College's new swimming complex, recently completed by Hopkins Architects. The new pool incorporates a moveable floor, allowing it to be used for water polo, diving, races and – of course – teaching.

BATHING REGULATIONS AT ATHENS

Fifth Form Nants in First Hundred and Upper and Middle Divisions may bathe at Athens. No bathing at Athens on Sundays after 8.30 a.m. At Athens, boys who are undressed must either get at once into the water or get behind screens when boats containing ladies come in sight. Boys when bathing are not allowed to land on the Windsor Bank or to swim out to launches and barges or to hang onto, or interfere with, boats of any kind. Any boy breaking this rule will be severely punished.

From School Rules of the River 1921

Address Along the Thames Path. what3words: chain.transmitted.motel | **Getting there** Train to either Windsor & Eton Riverside or Windsor & Eton Central, then a 25-minute walk; free parking at Boveney Ramblers Car Park (Dorney SL4 6QQ), followed by a 20-minute walk along the Thames Path | **Tip** Across the water, you catch a glimpse of Royal Windsor Racecourse. Where Ascot has Ladies' Day, Windsor hosts the equally glamorous Gents' Day. See the website for upcoming races: www.windsor-racecourse.co.uk.

10 Bachelors' Acre

Life and death in the people's playground

Look for the hidden alleyway along Peascod Street marked 'Acre Passage' and follow it down. In an instant, the hullabaloo of Windsor disappears as you find yourself in two acres (not one, as the name suggests) of peace and tranquillity.

Bachelors' Acre has seen a number of uses over the centuries. Shakespeare recorded the name as 'Pittie-ward', probably in reference to the lime pits that once littered the field. By 1615, it had taken on the name Bachelors' Acre. Some suspect this had something to do with women being banned from the area, but the 'Bachelors' in question were actually junior knights who came here to practise their archery.

In 1810, a group calling themselves the Bachelors of Windsor took it upon themselves to regenerate the area, which had gradually been turned into a sewage outlet for the surrounding houses. To celebrate their success, they threw on an ox roast to coincide with King George III's golden jubilee. The jubilee ox roast has since become a Bachelors' Acre tradition, with each festivity commemorated on an obelisk in the south-east corner.

One curious feature of the park is the graveyard, which was given to the parish church to house the overflow from their own cemetery. The most notable graves are those of Charles Knight sen. and jun., who co-founded the town's first weekly newspaper, *The Windsor and Eton Express*. The cemetery's lychgate was also installed in their honour.

Many people have tried and failed over the years to swipe Bachelors' Acre for themselves. The most notable attempt was in 1969, when the local council earmarked the site to be turned into a multi-storey car park. Thankfully, local woman Doris Mellor was 'aving none of it, and appealed directly to the High Court. Her success in that case ensured Bachelors' Acre will forevermore remain a recreation space – by the people of Windsor, for the people of Windsor.

Address Bachelors' Acre, Windsor SL4 1HE | Getting there Train to either Windsor & Eton Central or Windsor & Eton Riverside, then a 10-minute walk ; bus 1, W1, 2, 4, 7, 8, 16, 440, 702 or 703; car via B3022 to Victoria Street, nearby parking at Victoria Street Car Park | Tip Doris Mellor is commemorated around Windsor in a number of ways. 83 Peascod Street is named Mellor House and has a plaque bearing her portrait, while the road leading from Bachelors' Acre to the Windsor Library is named Mellor Walk.

11 Boots Passage
A prescription for urban renewal

If you were going to give a gift to King Edward VII, what would it be? Well, if you were Jesse Boot, of *Boots* pharmacy fame, you'd give… an alleyway. Yes, in 1921, Boot donated this side street running past his shop on Thames Street to the king and people of Windsor. With the official name of the King Edward VII Gateway (but still Boots Passage to the locals), it came with a bust of the king and a re-creation of Wenceslaus Hollar's 17th-century map of Windsor Castle. The king's reaction is not officially recorded, but you can imagine the look on his face.

So, why did Boot donate an alley of all things? The clue is illustrated on Hollar's map. Draw your eyes around the perimeter of the castle and you'll notice the cramped cluster of houses cloistered around the walls. Having been built over many centuries, when the words 'town planning' were still a long way off, Thames Street was until the 19th century a row of ramshackle buildings smushed together without rhyme or reason. We owe it to Robert Richard Tighe for cleaning up Windsor's main artery in the 1850s – he campaigned furiously to remove some of the more egregious properties, in turn giving the people of Windsor uninterrupted views of the castle from street level.

Boot continued Tighe's legacy with his choice gift. His passage allowed citizens to divert from Thames Street to Windsor's designated urban lungs, The Goswells and Alexandra Gardens (that it also funnelled people past his shop window was a happy coincidence). As you follow the path today, be sure to peek back over your shoulder – the view of the Curfew Tower is stunning, and a fitting testament to Tighe's vision. Better still, pop into the upstairs gallery of The King and Castle, a pub based in what was once Boot's Windsor branch. If you're lucky, you can grab the table directly above the snicket, offering a striking view in the other direction.

Address Look for the entrance beneath The King and Castle, 16–17 Thames Street, Windsor SL4 1PL | Getting there Train to either Windsor & Eton Central or Windsor & Eton Riverside, then a five-minute walk; served by most bus routes | Tip The Goswells at the bottom of the hill, which was converted from a slum to a meadow, is well worth a stop off. Follow the traditional lantern-style street lamps past the tennis courts and bowling green to discover the Jubilee Fountain opposite the gates to Alexandra Gardens.

12 Boulter's Lock & Ray Mill Island

A sculpture park in the Thames

Throughout the 1800s, dandies and dames converged on Boulter's Lock for the unofficial Ascot Week after-party. So animated was the scene, it inspired Edward John Gregory to paint *Boulter's Lock, Sunday Afternoon,* depicting a horde of racegoers funnelling their gondolas through the lock's bottleneck.

The setting is slightly less animated nowadays – more serene, I should say. In fact, the chief inhabitants of Ray Mill Island today seem to be its bronze statues. One of these is Eunice Goodman's *Maiden With Swans,* a namesake feature for the town inspired by scenes from medieval Maidenhead. Despite finishing second in a competition to become the island's official installation (behind Lydia Karpinska's *Vintage Boys,* who can be found lurking in the bushes nearby), local benefactor Richard Young loved the piece so much he funded the casting out of his own pocket. The piece was lovingly maintained until recently by Eunice's late husband Charles, who would visit every week armed with cleaning materials.

A second Goodman statue on the island is *The Companions.* The story behind this piece is, sadly, far more sombre. The Altwood Boy, as he is named, symbolises four young Maidenhead pupils who died tragically in a 1988 hiking accident. What is even sadder is that the statue is a replacement. The original was stolen in 2011 by some utter bast… ahem, *bad people.*

I will leave you to explore the rest of the island yourself. Make a stop at The Waterside Inn to watch the passing river over a sunset drink. On the other side of the island, watch the brave kayakers challenging the wash of Boulter's Weir. There is even an aviary – totally free to visit, and home to an eclectic mix of cockatiels, budgerigars and guinea pigs. Huh. Maybe the island is still animated after all.

Address Lower Cookham Road, Maidenhead SL6 8PE | **Getting there** Train to Maidenhead (Elizabeth Line), then bus 6 or 53 to Maidenhead Bridge followed by a 15-minute walk; pay and display parking at Boulter's Lock Car Park (SL6 8JN) | **Hours** Ray Mill Island: daily 7am–8.30pm; The Boathouse at Boulter's Lock: Mon–Sat 9am–11pm, Sun 9.30am–10.30pm | **Tip** Finish your visit with a stroll down Lower Cookham Road, known as the 'Thames Riviera', to drink in the vistas of both the beautiful houses and the historic Maidenhead Bridge.

13 — Bracknell New Town Mural
A landmark on a car park

Of all the villages in the former Great Forest, Bracknell is arguably the most successful. Much of this success is thanks to the fact it was chosen by Clement Attlee's post-World War II government to be designated a 'New Town'.

In order to accommodate the swelling population at the time, it was deemed necessary to rip down Bracknell's ancient High Street and replace it with modern concrete buildings. This proved an immensely unpopular decision, and the authority in charge of the project, Bracknell Development Corporation, had to work hard to keep people on side. Thus they commissioned renowned sculptor William Mitchell to design this huge mural, showing Bracknell's journey from Great Forest outpost to bustling New Town.

Faced in what is now well-weathered bronze, you can trace Bracknell's story as you read the mural left to right: prehistoric barrows, Roman standards and Saxon ships show who has inhabited the land since 1,200 B.C.; we then turn to Easthampstead Park, built for Edward III in 1350, which was a popular lodge for monarchs who wanted to get away from Windsor Castle – Henry VII is shown to be one of them, as is Catherine of Aragon, who stayed here both before her marriage and after her divorce from Henry VIII; Bracknell then develops into a thriving market town, renowned for its horse fairs, bull-baiting, egg auctions and most of all its sprawling brickyards; the mural ends with Bracknell New Town's radical rectangular skyscrapers juxtaposed against antique trees and churches.

Despite their efforts, the development corporation couldn't convince people to love the New Town, which was demolished in 2013 to make way for a new shopping centre. Thankfully, the mural was spared the same fate and, after a campaign by local residents, was restored to this car park overlooking Holy Trinity, the church that established Bracknell as its own parish in 1851.

Address Braccan Walk Car Park, The Ring, Bracknell RG12 1DR | **Getting there** Train to Bracknell; bus 4, 53, 108, 150, 151, 151A, 156, 157, 158, 171, 172, 194, 299, 412, 703 or X 94 to Bracknell Bus Station | **Tip** Fans of 20th-century art and architecture will find plenty to admire in Bracknell, but perhaps the most iconic structure is Point Royal (Rectory Lane, Bracknell RG12 7HJ), a 17-storey tower block designed by Arup Associates, which was used as a backdrop in Sean Connery's 1973 film *The Offence*.

14__Bray

Worth a special journey, says Michelin

Of the eight Michelin stars in the Royal Borough, seven of them are in Bray. Heston Blumenthal is responsible for four: three for The Fat Duck, one for The Hind's Head. The Waterside Inn, also with three, holds the British record for having been in every issue of the Michelin Guide. (FYI, the borough's eighth star is at Coworth Park – see ch. 21.)

But Bray does not need me to advertise its already world-renowned restaurants. Instead, let me offer this treasure hunt of interesting tit-bits around the village. The first thing to see is St Michael's Church, from where the legend of the 'Vicar of Bray' originates. This is not any one person in particular, rather a character who has entered folklore as an idiom for flip-flopping. The Vicar of Bray was said to change his allegiance from papist to protestant depending on which one the monarch at the time preferred. The story is depicted on an inscription in The Hind's Head.

Embedded in the wall of the church is a chunk of metal that local legend claims was a cannonball shot at the village during the Civil War. Inside the church are the coat of arms of James I, dated from 1604, which mercifully – and rather unusually – survived the Civil War unscathed.

Behind the church is St Michael's Hall. Keep an eye peeled for the stone carving representing a hound, believed to have come from the original Saxon church building. From here, head towards the Lich Gate on Church Lane. Notice the small inscription in the timber, which reads '1448' in Arabic numerals – the 'half' figures of eight are actually number fours.

Finally, at the other end of the High Street, stop by Jesus Hospital. The wardens, Jim and Betty Jackson, have established a museum of various artefacts found from this Grade I-listed, 17th-century building. Of particular note is the old guest book, signed by Charlie Chaplin and a litany of other revered names.

Address High Street, Bray, Maidenhead SL6 2AR | Getting there By car, follow the M4 then the B3028 | Tip One more thing to mention is the billiards table at Bray Village Hall, donated by Sir Hugo Cunliffe-Owen in 1923. It was dismantled and hidden in St Michael's Hall during the war, and the underside was graffitied by the men from the village who carted it across the village.

15 The Brocas

Picture-perfect view

Every local in Windsor has a place to go for a great view of the castle. For me, it's The Brocas. I am in good company, historically speaking. J. M. W. Turner, Alfred de Breanski, Gilbert Munger and Sanford Robinson Gifford all painted Windsor Castle from this meadow. A postcard found by one local historian even claims that the first photograph of Windsor Castle was taken here.

Why is the view from The Brocas so special? Probably because it is the only vista that includes all the major Thames-fronting bastions of the castle in one panorama. From left to right you have Brunswick Tower, King George IV Tower, Winchester Tower, the mighty Round Tower in the middle, then King Edward III Tower, the spires atop St George's Chapel, and the belfry of Curfew Tower just visible over the trees. Top tip: look for the flagpole on top of the Round Tower. On days where the red, blue and gold Royal Standard is flying, it means the king is in residence.

Despite passing through many hands over the years, arriving ultimately in the possession of Eton College, the field remains named after Sir John Brocas. As Master of the King's Horse, and with the help of his brother Arnold, John equipped Edward III's armies with mighty destriers, the strongest war horse of the era, which proved pivotal in campaigns against France and Scotland. Later retiring into the role of Chief Ranger of Windsor Forest, John invested his earnings in land, managing to scoop this brilliant portion of earth in the process – although, given its tendency for flooding, it's no wonder neither he, nor any subsequent owners, chose to build here.

Thus, the meadow remains more or less unchanged since those early days. In fact, perhaps the only things missing are the ferry ports that once took people over the river to Windsor, and the 40mm anti-aircraft gun that was mounted here during World War II.

Address Eton SL4 6BS | Getting there Train to Windsor & Eton Riverside, then cross Windsor Bridge, or to Windsor & Eton Central and a five-minute walk | Tip The ferrymen who worked this stretch of the Thames would later retire to the Watermans Arms, which dates from 1682. As well as classic pub fare, they serve up an excellent range of vegan meals.

16 — Burnham Abbey

Where sisters are still doing it for themselves

Burnham Abbey may have started life as early as 1263, but was not *officially* established until 1266. The reason for this is that the founder – Richard, Earl of Cornwall – had to spend those interim years as a prisoner of war after getting himself captured at the Battle of Lewes. Legend has it Richard's captor, Simon de Montfort, only released him on the proviso he would finish the damned abbey he'd been going on about during his three years in prison.

Since the abbey had been built in Richard's absence, he returned to find it had managed to piss a lot of people off. The land he'd given, which he thought was an unused part of his Cippenham estate (see ch. 19), was actually high-quality farmland that the locals of Burnham had been using. Furthermore, in order to ensure the abbey had a water source, Richard had given permission to divert a nearby stream, which had in turn caused Burnham's water source to run dry.

Despite its bad reputation, Burnham Abbey was one of the few convents to survive the Reformation relatively intact. Sure, the abbess and her nine nuns were kicked out, and the chapel was demolished, but the rest of this 13th-century building found a new lease of life as a farm. The site later fell into disrepair, but was restored by architect James Lawrence Bissley in 1913. Three years later, the abbey received its first monastic residents since 1539, in the form of the Society of the Precious Blood. Over the last century, this sisterhood has worked hard to restore Burnham Abbey back to full working order as an Augustinian nunnery, even going so far as to rebuild the chapel.

Much of the original 13th-century building remains amidst the modern restorations. Look out especially for the ruinous north wall – the last extant reminder of the original chapel – as well as the arched doorway of the Chapter House and the lancet windows of the infirmary.

Address Lake End Road, Taplow SL6 0PW, www.burnhamabbey.org | **Getting there**
By car, from Eton, follow Eton Wick Road onto Common Road, onto Lake End Road
(B3026) | **Hours** This is an active nunnery, so open days are rare (see website for details),
but there are many ways to view the abbey from a respectable distance, including from
an adjacent footpath | **Tip** Be careful if driving across Dorney Common. This area is still
registered as common land for grazing, which means cows have right of way over traffic. If
one decides to park itself in the middle of the road – as they often do – you know what to
shout: 'Moo-ove over!'

17__Cheapside

Where Windsor's working class lived

This Dairylea-shaped village occupies what is surely one of the most precious parcels of land in the borough, bounded by the Great Park on one side, Ascot Heath on the other, Sunninghill Park to the north and Silwood Park – now a campus of Imperial College London – to the south. Ironically, given the current price of property, this village was historically home to a community of the Great Forest's labourers. Presented today in much the same shape and, in some places, the same style as it has existed for hundreds of years, it offers a valuable look back at how the 'commoners' of the Great Forest lived and worked.

Post-Conquest, this part of the forest was divvied up between local élites, who fenced off parts of their land. Cheapside – named as such because it was, literally, the 'cheap side' – was swallowed up by the royal enclosure of Sunninghill Park, with the mighty manor house in the centre changing hands several times over the following centuries. Ordinary housing developed slowly, with the earliest homes clustered around The Thatched Tavern pub. The Enclosure of Windsor Forest Act of 1813 opened the land up to a grab-and-take, and growth accelerated as folk – often skilled labourers with job titles like plumber, glazier or chimney sweep – flooded into the area to build their own cottages, along with a school, a chapel and all the other village essentials that make Cheapside the idyllic suburb it is today.

I can hardly do the long history of this village justice in one page, so if you'd like to learn more I suggest picking up a copy of Christine Weightman's *Cheapside in the Forest of Windsor* from Chapmans Ironmongers in Sunninghill. Better yet, pop down for a stroll around this charming outpost. Keep an eye out for some historic homes squished between the more recent additions, and be sure to pop into 'The Thatch' to rub shoulders with the locals.

Address Cheapside Road, Ascot SL5 7QG | **Getting there** Bus 1 to Hilltop Close or 28 to Dorian Drive | **Tip** Integral to the history of this village is the nearby church of St Michael and All Angels (Sunninghill SL5 7DD). Established in the year A.D. 890, the present, ivy-clad tower is the work of William Henry Crossland and dedicated to Thomas Holloway, who was buried here.

18 Cinnamon Café

All roads lead to bun

There are several stunning routes from London to Windsor by bike. The most popular is National Route 4, 'the Thames Path', which carries riders along the idyllic riverside with time for a spin in Richmond Park, ending in a long, flat sprint through Runnymede. Then there is the Grand Union Canal towpath, a tour of North West London's industrial heartlands, all 90-degree turns and sickeningly steep bridge climbs, turning off at Langley in time for a view of the Castle from Upton Court Park.

Meanwhile, courageous road cyclists prefer the fast-paced metropolitan route of the A4, a noodle soup of three-lane carriageways that goes under the bellies of planes making the short final descent into Heathrow. Whichever route the chain gang chooses, one thing is guaranteed: their journey will end, stiff-calved and low-blood-sugared, on the terrace of Cinnamon Café.

Enter through the red brick archway. Order the cinnamon bun so good they named the business after it. Now look around. Have you ever seen a café quite like this? As you might have guessed, this tile-walled, parquet-floored nook with its gorgeous, wooden vaulted ceiling was never intended to be a coffee shop. Rather, it was the post room and ticket hall of Windsor Royal Station. The concourse has receded over the years, but the sublime Victorian architecture remains, and Cinnamon Café takes full advantage.

Make no mistake, this unit is coveted: international chains have tried, and failed, to swoop on this space. In 2017, the Windsor community fought back against such plans by launching a petition that garnered thousands of signatures. Many of the signatories were cyclists who consider Cinnamon hallowed ground, the terminus of a pilgrimage known as the 'Bun Run'. Indeed, the 25-mile ride from London can only be deemed finished the moment the peckish peloton tucks into their tasty wedge of cinnamon bun.

Address Unit 53, Windsor Royal Station, Jubilee Arch, Windsor SL4 1PJ, +44 (0)1753 857879, www.cinnamoncafe.com | **Getting there** Round the corner from Windsor & Eton Central Station, or a five-minute walk from Windsor & Eton Riverside Station | **Hours** Daily 7.15am–6pm | **Tip** If you're day-tripping around Windsor, you're in the right place. The other half of Cinnamon Café's unit is the Royal Windsor Information Centre. Help yourself to some free literature while you enjoy your coffee.

19 Cippenham Moat

When Slough was home to kings

If you needed proof that history can be found in the most unlikely of places, here we are, outside an Asda, in the middle of a housing estate just off the M4. Stay with me. I promise it gets better.

As the lie of the land hints, something pretty monumental used to exist here. Trace a path around the curious soil banks, and you can just about make it out: a square moat, with an earth bridge running through the middle towards what would have been a royal palace. And not just any royal palace, but that of the King of the Romans himself, Richard, Earl of Cornwall.

This ancient palace played an interesting role in one of the 13th-century's greatest scandals. Richard was brother to King Henry III and, as can be quite typical in heir-and-spare relationships, the two brothers did not get on. This came to a head in 1231, when Richard hastily married the wealthy widow Isabel Marshal, much to the chagrin of his brother, who had wanted to marry his brother off to some continental princess. The newlyweds eloped to Cippenham while the heat died down, although thankfully Henry didn't seem to care too much – he probably felt sorry for Isabel, given his brother's reputation for womanising.

Richard died in 1272, and the palace at Cippenham disappeared shortly after. The only thing that remains are these earthworks, later discovered by Victorian farmers. All this really begs the question, how did the palace get here in the first place? Samuel Lewis, in his 1848 *A Topographical Dictionary of England*, posited that it was built for the kings of Mercia, but that idea was pooh-poohed by historians who could find no hard evidence. That was until 2016, when nearby Montem Mound (see ch. 61) was found to be of Saxon origin, opening up the discussion once again.

If the legend is true, we may soon have to acquiesce that it is Slough, not Windsor, that is the true seat of royal power in England.

Address Wood Lane, Slough SL1 9JB, www.cippenham.org | Getting there Bus 5 to Braemar Gardens | Tip It's not the most scenic of places, but what better way to round off your historical odyssey to Slough than with a visit to the adroitly named Earl of Cornwall pub?

20__Copper Horse's Stirrups
Or lack thereof

As magnificent as it is, ask a local Windsorian about this famous statue and you may get a sombre reaction, for *The Copper Horse* is associated with a harrowing urban myth.

While visiting for yourself, take a look at King George III's stirrups and you'll spot something peculiar. They're not there! The story goes that the sculptor, Sir Richard Westmacott, forgot to include them and only noticed his omission after the statue was unveiled in 1821. So ashamed was he of his mistake, he took himself into the forest and hanged himself from a tree.

How chilling. How tragic. But also, what a load of horse manure. I am pleased to tell you Sir Richard had a long and illustrious career before passing away in 1856 at the ripe old age of 81. Neither is the apparent mistake a mistake at all – the statue is intended to mimic an ancient sculpture of a similarly stirrup-less Marcus Aurelius. Sir Richard trained as a sculptor in Rome, and was very much a follower of the classical style. In fact, look a little closer and you'll see King George donning a laurel wreath and toga – both a reflection of the sculptor's tastes, and intended to symbolise the connection between the British and Roman empires.

Why then the myth? Well, it seems someone may have mixed the story of *The Copper Horse* up with that of Herne the Hunter (see ch. 39). Herne was a legendary hunter who was cursed by a wizard and hanged himself from a tree in the Windsor Great Forest. Perhaps it also had something to do with the fact that *The Copper Horse* was damaged *en route* to the Great Park and one of the legs had to be replaced. Or maybe the rumour was started by George IV, who famously despised his father – despite commissioning this statue in his memory.

Whatever the case, that's one folk tale put out to pasture. Next up, why is it called *The Copper Horse* when it was made from 25 tons of brass salvaged from old cannons?

Address Long Walk, Windsor Great Park, Windsor SL4 2HW | **Getting there** Nearest public parking is at Bishopsgate Road, Englefield Green TW20 0XU, then a 20-minute walk. Ranger's Gate Car Park (SL4 2LD) and Cranbourne Gate Car Park (SL4 2BT) are both a 30-minute walk away. | **Tip** Divert west from the Long Walk to the Review Ground, where you can walk among ancient oak trees. One in particular to look out for is the Signing Oak, believed to be around 1,000 years old. A digitally-created, bronze scale model of the tree by studio Factum Arte was gifted to Queen Elizabeth II for her 90th birthday.

21__Coworth Park

The Great Park's boujie neighbour

The hardest thing when describing Coworth Park is to avoid using that old cliché 'rustic charm'. You'd think it would be easy – this estate is owned by the city-slicking Dorchester Collection, better known for achieving the rarest feat in a game of Monopoly by sticking two hotels on London's Park Lane. Yet 'rustic charm' is the only description that does the job. Because it is rustic: the complex evolved from the hamlet of Coworth, which appeared on John Norden's 1607 map of Windsor Forest, and retains many of the village-y features that make it feel less like a hotel, more like a farmstead – a red phone box, its own milestone, a meadow producing food for the kitchens. So too is it charming: this is the only hotel in the UK where you can learn to play polo, on one of the hotel's own horses, which are often seen clopping past the lime grove as cars cruise by at the designated speed limit of nine and a half miles per hour.

The illusion of homeliness is only broken when you step into one of the grand maisons, for there you are greeted with the kind of opulence that seems to whisper 'money means nothing'. It has taken a millennium-long journey to arrive at this level of grandeur, spanning several high-profile owners beginning with Edward the Confessor, via William Shepheard who built the Georgian mansion, ending most recently with Galen Weston, former owner of Selfridges.

In that time, Coworth Park has played host to countless distinguished guests, for whom it made the perfect base from which to get to Windsor and the Ascot races. Many of the guests who stay today are equally as distinguished and come for the same things. This time, however, they have the options of Michelin-starred cuisine from chef Adam Smith, a swim in the sunken spa, or a stay in one of the farmhouses where they can experience the full force of that – argh, there's that cliché again – rustic charm.

Address Blacknest Road, Sunningdale SL5 7SE, +44 (0)1344 876600, www.dorchestercollection.com/coworth-park | Getting there Look for signs along Blacknest Road (A329), parking on site | Hours Afternoon tea: daily 12.30–4.30pm; Woven by Adam Smith: dinner Wed–Sat 6.30–9pm, lunch Sat & Sun 12.30–2pm; The Barn: lunch daily 12.30–2pm, dinner daily 6–9pm; Bar: daily noon–11pm; Spa: daily 7am–9pm | Tip Foodies are in the right neck of the woods, as just up the road is the Michelin-recommended Bluebells (www.bluebells-restaurant.co.uk).

22 The Crooked House
The leaning tower of Windsor

It's a testament to our ability to find beauty in the unconventional that Windsor's Crooked House (Market Cross House, to use its proper name) has become one of the town's most Instagrammed locations. It is the very definition of quirky, all poky and rickety both inside and out. From the outside, the nine degree tilt is most pronounced at the rear, where the back door leans dramatically into the bay window. Inside, the building is as vertigo-inducing as Jamiroquai's 'Virtual Insanity'. It is, in these respects, the perfect location for its current tenant, The Shambles Bar. I dare you to try and make it to the toilet on the second floor after a couple of their locally sourced bottles.

According to local legend, the peculiar constitution of this building owes its history to a rather hilarious balls-up. It started with the demolition of the Market Cross and its replacement with the Windsor Guildhall in 1690 (see ch. 59). One unexpected casualty in this project was that the original Market Cross House – then home to a butcher's, which may have had a secret tunnel from their shop to the castle's kitchen – was accidentally knocked down. The tenants raised a stink, and the builders were forced to rebuild their house. However, with no neighbouring structures to lean on, and with the new timber frames made out of unseasoned green oak, no sooner was construction finished than the building started to lean. Thankfully, when the wood hardened, the building became more stable, and has remained standing ever since.

One happy coincidence from this fudged restoration was that it created the dainty Queen Charlotte Street alongside. While it declares itself Britain's shortest street, I am afraid to say that claim is somewhat unfounded. At 51 feet and 10 inches, it is at least 34 feet longer than Elgin Street in Bacup, and 44 feet longer than Ebenezer Place in Wick.

Address 51 High Street, Windsor SL4 1LR, www.theshamblesbar.co.uk | Getting there Train to either Windsor & Eton Central or Windsor & Eton Riverside, then a five-minute walk; served by most bus routes | Hours Wed & Thu 10am–11pm, Fri & Sat 10am–midnight, Sun 10am–8pm | Tip Market Cross House is sometimes referred to as the oldest tea room in England. Just round the corner, you'll find Clarence Tea Room, which may not be as old, but could certainly lay a claim to being one of the best.

23 Death Warrant of Charles I

A king's consequence

The Civil War decimated the population of England, pitting brothers against brothers on the field of battle. After Oliver Cromwell and his New Model Army won a decisive victory in 1645, King Charles I fled to Scotland, leaving the question of who ruled England unanswered. At a meeting at Windsor Castle in April 1648, Cromwell and his supporters decided enough was enough. It was time, in their own words, 'to call Charles Stuart, that man of blood, to an account for that blood he had shed'.

Charles was brought from Scotland to Caversham Court to await trial. Fearing the worst, he was allowed to make one brief journey into Maidenhead to bid farewell to his children at the Greyhound Inn. From there, he continued to London, where the High Court of Justice found him guilty of treason and sentenced him to death. A warrant for the execution was hastily drawn up and signed by 59 members of the Rump Parliament. Local legend suggests the final signatories added their names at Curfew Yard opposite Windsor Castle.

On the bitterly cold afternoon of 30 January, 1649, a scaffold was erected outside Banqueting House, Whitehall. 'I go from a corruptible to an incorruptible crown,' Charles uttered as his final words. 'Where no disturbance can be, no disturbance in the world.' With that, he raised one arm, signalling the executioner to drop his axe. His head was lopped off in one fell swoop, as the crowd below him groaned – in executing the king, Cromwell had betrayed the very laws he had sworn to uphold.

With his head sewn back onto his body, Charles was buried at St George's Chapel. Many years later, a copy of his death warrant appeared on a pub in Church Street, aptly named Ye Olde King's Head. Its choice of location, mere yards away from the home of the royal family, offers a poignant reminder that being a king or queen is not always fun and games.

Address 7 Church Street, Windsor SL4 1PE | Getting there Train to either Windsor & Eton Central or Windsor & Eton Riverside, then a five-minute walk; served by most bus routes | Tip If gin's your thing, you're in the right part of the world. Not only does Windsor Castle produce its own variety, which can be found in the gift shop (when it's not already snapped up), the adjacent Queen Charlotte pub stocks more than 150 varieties of the spirit.

24 Deer Park
The Great Park's stag party

The king may claim to own the Great Park, but really he just leases it from the deer. These majestic creatures have been here since long before he, or any other royal arrived – in fact, they have been around since before the Great Park was the Great Park. So significant is their presence, their patriarch – the stag – has become the symbol of Berkshire, represented on its flag, its coat of arms, and in the names of countless pubs (see ch. 72 and ch. 80).

The Deer Park is, in name, the last vestige of the royal hunting ground known as Windsor Great Forest. In medieval times, royal huntsmen would chase deer through these woods on horseback. By night, they would rest in the many hunting lodges dotted throughout – especially if they wanted to avoid the spirit of Herne the Hunter (see ch. 39).

These hunting lodges helped to spur the development of towns and villages throughout the Great Forest. But, since only wealthy landowners were allowed to hunt, ordinary peasants had to eke out an income maintaining the deer for the pleasure of the upper classes. Of course, they weren't averse to poaching, especially during the English Civil War, when the deer population was decimated.

A fresh import of German and Scandinavian deer helped to save the stock from extinction, and even gave rise to a new breed called the 'Windsor Park' deer, which ironically are not the ones you'll see here today – they were all shipped over to Richmond Park in the 1950s and replaced with red deer from Balmoral.

These red deer now enjoy a pampered lifestyle, looked after by the Great Park's gamekeepers. Do be mindful that these are wild animals, so don't try to get too close. And beware especially the autumn months: this is the rutting season, when stags lock antlers in a battle for control of the hinds. Believe me. You don't want to get in the way of a, erm, *stag's horn*.

Address Egham TW20 0XY | Getting there Nearest parking at Savill Garden Car Park (Wick Lane, Englefield Green TW20 0UU), then a 25-minute walk. Follow signs through the Great Park towards the Deer Park. Always observe safety and accessibility advice at the gates. | Hours Daily dawn to dusk | Tip Head south-west from the Deer Park and follow Queen Anne's Ride, an avenue lined with over 1,000 oak trees, to the Queen Elizabeth II Golden Jubilee Statue. Sculpted by Philip Jackson, it was the first ever public statue of the late queen.

25 Dorney Court

If you like piña coladas, and old Tudor homes

Dorney Court has been the nucleus of local power in this part of the world since time immemorial. The Saxons named this land 'Island of Bumblebees', but even they might not have been the first to get here, as in 1996 archaeologists found the remains of prehistoric bridges and high-profile burials dating as far back as 1,300 B.C. Long after the Conquest, Dorney Court came into the possession of Sir Robert Lytton who built himself this fine Tudor house, later acquired by Sir William Garrard who added the adjacent church of St James the Less. James Palmer married Garrard's daughter, and the house has remained in the possession of the Palmer family ever since.

Dorney Court retains all the medieval charm that makes it so deserving of its Grade I-listed status, and can appropriately be called one of the finest extant Tudor homes in England. The brickwork is charmingly hotchpotch, the timber frames are an affront to spirit levels everywhere, and the grounds are landscaped to a tee. Inside, it's all dusty carpets and creaking floorboards, the walls decked in original oil paintings, the wainscoting barely illuminated by the natural light from the casement windows – and yet, there is one bit of decoration in the drawing room that manages to catch a glimmer: an inconspicuous bronze pineapple.

The pineapple is integral to the story of Dorney Court, for it is widely believed that here, in around 1677, the Royal Gardener John Rose cultivated the first such fruit in England. This momentous achievement came at a time when the pineapple was not for eating, no no; rather, it was for wealthy élites to display in their homes. Who better, then, to receive the first English pineapple than King Charles II? So historic was the occasion, one artist saw fit to paint the ceremonial presentation of the Dorney pineapple, in a piece that now hangs at Ham House, London.

Address Court Lane, Dorney SL4 6QP, +44 (0)1628 604638, www.dorneycourt.co.uk | Getting there Bus 63 or 69 | Hours Generally daily 12.30–4pm, but at certain times of year by appointment only – see website for details | Tip There's no other way to finish your tour than with a stop by the aptly-named, 15th-century pub The Pineapple, where you can enjoy a fantastic pizza (with pineapple, naturally).

26__Drury House

Where Charles II had his bit on the side

Over the centuries, Church Street has been the beating heart of what was once a sprawling 'shambles', Windsor's claustrophobic market hub. The cramped arrangement of houses is typical of a medieval castle town – narrow streets like these were intended to confuse and slow down advancing armies, giving peasants time to throw hot oil from their bedroom windows. Mind you, this road had a far more effective deterrent – it was originally named Fyssh Street, owing to the number of fishmongers who made their living here, with a smell zesty enough to put any invader off.

At the centre of this road, one building stands apart for its historical intrigue. 'Nell Gwyn's House' was allegedly built by King Charles II for his favourite mistress (for she was indeed one of many). Theirs was a romance worthy of a Disney movie: while performing one night on Drury Lane, Gwyn – a prostitute's daughter turned actress – caught the eye of Charles, who invited her for dinner. Like the gentleman he was, Charles split without paying the bill, but Gwyn was nothing if not persistent, pursuing the king and strong-arming her way into his harem. She lived the rest of her life moving from one scenic house to the next, with Charles delighting in finding ever more sly ways to arrange their *rendezvous*. For their liaisons at Windsor, the rumour mill posits Charles built a tunnel connecting Gwyn's house directly to the Castle.

Today, this tunnel is blocked off, used instead as a wine cellar by *The Cobbles*. Brought to you by Davi Ryatt and Monty Lal, this upmarket champagne bar makes fine use of the building's antique aesthetic – all dark wood walls and warped timber staircases – to provide an intimate setting in which to enjoy their locally sourced victuals. How's this for a marketing pitch: come and enjoy a glass of bubbly in the same room where a king and his mistress used to get down and dirty.

Address 4 Church Street, Windsor SL4 1PE, www.thecobbleswindsor.co.uk | Getting there Train to either Windsor & Eton Central or Windsor & Eton Riverside, then a five-minute walk; served by most bus routes | Hours Summer noon–11pm daily, winter 5–11pm daily | Tip Cramped medieval roads like Church Street were notorious tinderboxes, and sure enough a great fire in the early 1800s gutted a large part of this area. The ruins of one unfortunate house can still be seen in the corner of Church Street Gardens.

27 Egham Museum
The human side of local history

With its parish borders incorporating Runnymede, Egham is the official town of Magna Carta. It would, therefore, have been easy for Egham Museum to fashion itself entirely around this event. However, the curators have looked far beyond Magna Carta to create a museum that shows how people, rather than circumstances, have shaped Egham's urban history.

One manifestation of this theme is in the tale of Lady Fairhaven. When the raucous Egham Races came to an end in 1888, Runnymede Meadow fell into the crosshairs of property developers. In a bid to protect this historic land, the philanthropic Fairhaven donated her share to the National Trust, thus safeguarding it for future generations.

Then there is Thomas Holloway, founder of the multi-million pound enterprise Holloway's Pills and Ointments. He used his fortune to build two institutions that, thanks to their wonderful architecture (the work of William Henry Crossland), have made Egham a destination in its own right: Holloway Sanitorium, a mental health hospital, and the Founder's Building of Holloway College, now Royal Holloway University.

These are just two of the people that Egham Museum brings to life through its collection of clippings, photographs and oral testimonies. But there are hundreds more artefacts to tell the story of ordinary Eghamites who have stamped their mark on this town.

Start with the Bronze Age finds, which show how humans have lived in this space since 10,000 B.C. Admire the old village stocks, which one prankster graffitied 'Cromwell for Pope'. See the coat of World War II evacuee Colin Ryder-Richardson, whose mother sewed a life jacket into the seams. The sense you will be left with is not that Egham has played silent witness to centuries of history, but that it has relentlessly carved out its own.

Address The Literary Institute, 51 High Street, Egham TW20 9EW, +44 (0)1784 434483, www.eghammuseum.org | **Getting there** Train to Egham; bus 8, 8B, 440, 441, 442, 500 or 656 to Church Road | **Hours** Tue, Thu & Sat 10.30am–1pm | **Tip** Time your visit on the Saturday closest to 15 June to experience Magna Carta Day, a local festival commemorating the signing of the charter of 1215.

28 Englemere Pond

The train will not be calling at Windsor or Ascot

As the town of Ascot becomes ever more desirable to wealthy expats from the big city, parcels of land that have been spared the developer's clutches, and which have earned the title of protected nature reserve, are becoming hard to find. Thankfully, Englemere Pond has survived the creep of modernity, much to the satisfaction of both local residents and the countless species of birds, insects and reptiles who call this tranquil sanctum home.

Yet, if history had had its way, this precious pocket of paradise might not have lived to tell the tale. Once upon a time, this area was scheduled to become part of the Windsor to Ascot railway, a scheme that, after countless failed starts, ultimately came to nought.

The first proposal came in 1870, with the idea to build a fork at the southern end of the Windsor Railway Bridge (see ch. 106) to carry passengers through Clewer, Datchet and Cranbourne, and onwards to Ascot Racecourse with a terminus at Englemere Pond. An updated proposal in 1877 went one step further: instead of stopping at Englemere, the line would continue south to connect with the railway to Aldershot, forming a sprawling railway junction in the middle of the forest. Subsequent proposals saw the line extended to Fifield and Winkfield, and a final proposal in 1898 even proposed multiple snaking lines through Ascot with various stations dotted around the racecourse.

However, cracks in the plan appeared faster than renewed proposals could cover them up. Local opposition proved a powerful force, and the cost of purchasing some of the most expensive land in the country drove the total budget to over £10 million in today's money. The Windsor & Ascot Railway Company officially formed in 1898, only to dissolve a year later when it was evident they would never be able to fund the project, and the scheme was finally put out of its misery on 9 December, 1911.

Address Swinley Road, Ascot SL5 8AB | Getting there Train to Ascot, then a 20-minute walk; the above postcode will take you to the free car park on Swinley Road (B3017) | Tip On the other side of Swinley Road is Whitmoor Bog. Every December, this forest plays host to Lapland UK, a fully-immersive Christmas experience – booking ahead essential (www.laplanduk.co.uk).

29_Eton College Wall

And you thought the offside rule was weird

A stimulating atmosphere stirs around Eton College on the dawn of St Andrew's Day. The boys put on their uniforms as usual, but they're not headed to lessons. Instead, they rush to climb the iron rungs jutting out of this brick wall on Slough Road. Before long, the entire length is lined with boys in tailcoats looking down at the Furrow (the 16-foot wide 'pitch') and the Calxes (the 'goals'). It's time for the Wall Game to begin.

The Oppidan team struts up Slough Road in purple and salmon shirts; the Colleger team, in purple and white, awaits them on the Furrow. The challenge is issued when the Oppidans toss their hats over the wall, before themselves jumping over like invaders storming a castle. The Collegers march, arm-in-arm, to meet them. An umpire greets the captains: 'You know the rules', he says. 'No furking. No sneaking. And certainly no knuckling.' The captains nod, and a coin is flipped. The winning captain chooses to shoot at either the Good (towards the door) or Bad (towards the tree) Calx, and then it's time to form the Bully (the 'scrum'). One boy kneels on the ball, and a struggle ensues, both teams grappling and shoving until the ball breaks loose, at which point a Line ('field player') rushes forward, grabs the ball, and boots it off the field.

On and on it goes like this until a boy gets close enough to the end of the Furrow to attempt a 'Shy', which he achieves by carrying the ball over the line and crying 'Got it!' He can then throw (worth nine points) or kick (five points) the ball against the Calx. But this is a moot point, for rarely is a point ever scored – every game since 1909 has finished 0–0. After 55 minutes the final whistle blows, leaving ordinary spectators looking around for clues as to what the hell they just witnessed. The answer? An Eton tradition from time immemorial, as absurd a spectacle today as it's always been.

Address Slough Road, Windsor SL4 6HD, www.etoncollege.com | **Getting there** Train to Windsor & Eton Riverside or Windsor & Eton Central, then a 15-minute walk; bus 15, 63 or 68 to Eton College, then head north for five minutes on Slough Road | **Tip** A little further north on Slough Road is a bridge over Colenorton Brook. From here, you can get a view of Eton College Chapel so spectacular it inspired J. M. W. Turner to paint it in watercolour.

30__Fortescues

A Windsor legacy, reimagined

Ice cream is probably not the first thing that comes to mind when you think of Windsor. But it was here, in 1671, that King Charles II became the first person to sample this chilly treat on British shores. At the Feast of St George, Charles polished off his meal with a banquet of tasty treats including a dish of Chinese oranges, three plates of liquid sweetmeats, and a mysterious item that has since become a staple of the British diet: one plate of ice cream. So momentous was the occasion, all the other guests turned to watch the king wolf down his serving.

That momentous occasion would go on to have a profound effect on English architecture. When upper-class gourmets learned of this fashionable new dessert, they knew they had to have it for themselves. However, ice was hard to come by in those days. It first had to be 'harvested', which meant bringing it from the icy tundras of Scandinavia by boat. Then, it needed to be stored, and of course at a low enough temperature to stop it from melting. To that end, wealthy homeowners would construct 'ice houses' within the confines of their country manors – deep underground chambers where the naturally chilly climate kept the ice solid well into summer.

You don't need to go to such efforts today. Instead, make a beeline for Fortescues. Since opening in 2021, this boutique *gelateria* founded by mum-dad-daughter team Joannie, Thomas and Olivia Peak has already become a Windsor institution, an essential whistlestop for those about to embark on a tour of the castle – and the place where Britain began its love affair with ice cream. And yes, I know ice cream and gelato aren't the same thing, don't @ me.

If you're lucky enough to grab a table outside on a hot day, be sure to order yours not in a cup or a cone, but the traditional Windsor way – on a plate, stacked with crumbled biscuit, and drizzled over with chocolate.

Address 13 Church Street, Windsor SL4 1PE, +44 (0)7971 243949, www.facebook.com/
FortescuesofWindsor | Getting there Train to either Windsor & Eton Central or
Windsor & Eton Riverside, then a five-minute walk; served by most bus routes | Hours
Daily 9am–6pm | Tip Overseas visitors may want to try the conventional British ice cream,
the '99 with Flake', also known as a 'Mr Whippy'. These are usually served from that Great
British institution, the ice cream van, but you'll also find them at Mamma Mia Café near
Windsor Promenade.

31 The Fred Fuzzens Plaque
Remembering a local legend

Blue plaques are, strictly speaking, a London phenomenon. The first blue plaques started popping up in the capital in 1867, commemorating places associated with persons of national interest. Thankfully, the scheme's proprietors English Heritage turn a blind eye to the unsexy issue of copyright, which has opened the door for local councils, societies and private individuals to stick up their own blue plaques. The community-run website www.openplaques.org lists over 17,000 plaques throughout the United Kingdom.

The Royal Borough of Windsor & Maidenhead has at least two dozen of its own. However, contrary to the way English Heritage does things, RBWM tends not to commemorate prominent Sirs and Madams – that would be too easy in a place like Windsor. Rather, it is local people who have made a difference who earn the coveted blue plaque.

One of those is Windsor's 'singing postman' Fred Fuzzens. Remembered with fondness by all who encountered him, Fuzzens' knowledge of the town – gleaned from walking a casual 20 miles a day delivering letters – was encyclopaedic. He put this knowledge to good use, contributing ten articles to local history periodical *Windlesora*. He was also known to go to the ends of the earth for the people of Windsor. When Dedworth Green needed a larger postbox, he got them one. When a retirement home in Clewer needed a sheltered bus stop, he got them one. And speaking of going to the ends of the earth, Fuzzens also attracted the attention of the *Bideford Gazette* in 1975 when he walked the 13 miles from Bideford to Buckland Brewer in the footsteps of his hero, the poet-postman Edward Capern.

In his 1997 obituary, *Windlesora* editor Pamela Marson recalled how when she first met Fuzzens she told him her name, and he responded by telling Pamela her address. May his plaque on Peascod Street's Post Office inspire us all to be heroes for our communities.

Royal Borough of Windsor and Maidenhead

FRED FUZZENS
1921 - 1995

A local man – He
strove for
a perfect
Windsor

Address 38–39 Peascod Street, Windsor SL4 1AA | **Getting there** Train to Windsor & Eton Central, then a five-minute walk, or to Windsor & Eton Riverside and a 10-minute walk; served by most bus routes | **Tip** Another notable blue plaque can be found at Oliphant House (9 Clarence Crescent SL4 5DT). This commemorates Scottish author and historian Margaret Oliphant who, in her 30 years at this house, produced no fewer than 60 works.

32 Frost Folly

Wildflowers and warblers in Warfield

The chirps of skylarks coming from their nests in the wildflower heaths combine with the humming of dragonflies fluttering through the hedgerows. Overhead, hungry red kites and courting goldfinches zoom around by day; by night, they are replaced by owls and bats. Meanwhile, in a small lake, frogs hunt for water boatmen between the stems of bulrushes.

It is as if all the species of the world have converged here, in this ubiquitous divot in the Warfield countryside. But make no mistake, Frost Folly is a rarity in this pastoral tract of land: being some of the prettiest land south of Windsor, Warfield has long been coveted by those who sought a home close to the Royal epicentre, and has thus become dominated by private estates and manor houses. The consequence of so much enclosure has been to exclude commoners like us from so much of Warfield's incredible countryside.

For breaking that mould, we have Jean Frost to thank. In 2003, she donated part of her estate in memory of her late husband, with the proviso that the parish council would maintain the land as a nature reserve. While the area has retained the couple's name, the 'Folly' is an enigma, this being a horizon quite devoid of any architectural features, unless we count the striking tower of St Michael's Church in the distance.

On that note, be sure to make this ancient church part of your circuit. Look for the 12th-century 'Devil's Door' on the north side, through which the Devil would be expelled after a baptism, and the 14th-century carving of the 'Green Man', a pagan symbol of resurrection and a rare sight in medieval churches in the carvings around the sedilia. Behind the church is the old rectory, once home to Sir William Herschel, who is credited as the first person to recognise the permanence of fingerprints, paving the way for the later invention of fingerprinting technology.

Address Weller's Lane, Warfield, Bracknell RG42 6EN | Getting there By car, follow the postcode on your satnav to the Frost Folly Car Park, which provides free parking from dawn till dusk | Tip Save some time for a stroll around Moss End Garden Village, just down the hill from the car park. Kids and parents could spend hours wandering between everything from an antiques store to a falconry centre, a pottery painting studio and an array of cafés.

33 Graves of Diana Dors and Alan Lake

Romeo and Juliet of the British film industry

A hellraiser of unusual beauty and god-given talent, Diana Fluck lied about her age to break into the acting world at just 14 years old under the surname 'Dors'. Her rise was meteoric. By her early twenties, she was one of Britain's busiest leading ladies, both on stage and on screen. Residencies in Hollywood followed, as did a few forays into singing.

But Dors was unlucky in love and, by extension, unlucky in money too. Her first husband, Dennis Hamilton, used his role as Dors' *de facto* agent to syphon money into his own back pocket. In time, Dors started an affair with Tommy Yeardye, and when she later fell for Richard Dawson instead, Yeardye responded by burgling Dors' safe. Marrying Dawson helped Dors break into America, but their divorce forced her to move back home without her two sons – and bankrupt, to boot.

While recouping her losses, Dors took a role in the short-lived TV series *The Inquisitors*. It was there she met her third and final husband, Alan Lake, and the two settled in a plush home in Sunningdale. Their relationship was stormy, marked by Lake's alcoholism and Dors' declining health. The ultimate tragedy was inevitable. Dors died of ovarian cancer in May 1984 and, five months later, an inconsolable Lake took his own life.

The pair are remembered with modest headstones in this unassuming cemetery. Dors' die-hard fans continue to pop by and pay their respects, often leaving behind memorabilia that remind us that these were no ordinary people, theirs was no ordinary love, and these are no ordinary graves.

One question remains: did Dors die penniless, or did she leave behind a coded message pointing the way to a hidden fortune? And could these graves play a part in unravelling the mystery? Alas, that's a story for another book…

Address Kiln Lane Cemetery, Kiln Lane, Sunningdale SL5 0LT, +44 (0)1344 874268, www.sunningdale-pc.org.uk/churches-and-cemetery | **Getting there** Train to Sunningdale, then a 25-minute walk; bus 1 to Sunningdale High Street; accessible by car via Kiln Lane, off the B383 (parking available) | **Tip** To complete your Diana Dors tour of Sunningdale, head up High Street then Bedford Lane. Dors and Lake lived in the charming Orchard Manor up Shrubbs Hill Lane, and worshipped at the adjacent Sacred Heart Catholic Church.

34 Guildhall Columns

Wren & Stumpy

Since 1690, the Guildhall has acted as the basin into which all of Windsor's civic history has flowed. This remains the case today – in fact quite literally, now that the Royal Borough Museum has become a tenant of the ground floor. But we're not here to talk about the Guildhall itself. Rather, we're here to talk about a local legend concerning the columns under the canopy.

Cast your eyes to the top of these columns and you'll notice there's about an inch of space between the capital and the ceiling above, rendering them rather obsolete. The urban myth in question attributes this curious fault to none other than Sir Christopher Wren, who had stepped in to oversee the final stages of construction after the Guildhall's original architect, Sir Thomas Fitch, passed away.

According to the legend, someone expressed concern the ceiling was going to collapse, and insisted Wren should install columns. Wren argued that the structure was perfectly sound without them, but the councillors pressured him to do it anyway. Wren obliged, but in a last act of defiance made them purposely too short. The quote-unquote 'mistake' went unnoticed until the 1800s, when a cleaner accidentally slipped his hand into one of the crevices.

Now, I have a theory about what happened next. When this cleaner reported the anomaly to the councillors at the time, they realised the construction of the Guildhall's 1829 extension might have caused the foundations underneath the building to subside. In order to keep this quiet – and to avoid taking the blame – they hastily concocted their own folk tale, which, to be fair, would have sounded somewhat plausible. That is, if you ignore the fact there's no evidence Sir Christopher Wren ever actually worked on the Guildhall – he was only brought in as a consultant, and was probably a little preoccupied with the rebuilding of London after the Great Fire of 1666!

Address High Street, Windsor SL4 1LR | Getting there Train to either Windsor & Eton Central or Windsor & Eton Riverside, then a five-minute walk; served by most bus routes | Hours Royal Borough Museum: Wed – Sun 10am – 4pm | Tip I hate to burst your bubble again, but the Guildhall was never actually a guildhall. No guild ever met here – they instead met next door at The Three Tuns pub, which has since been renamed The Prince Harry.

35 Hands-on Art

Interactive adventures in painting and pottery

I wonder how many tons of clay the knick-knack shops around Windsor Castle account for every year. I shouldn't comment – I have a real soft spot for tourist tat. But if the run-of-the-mill 'Made in China' fridge magnets and dinner plates aren't getting your kitsch glands stirring, Windsor has another option.

And what an option. Because I mean, who would settle for a generic 'I Heart Windsor' keyring, when they could have a pirate King Charles mecha robot wielding dual samurai swords? Or anything else for that matter – mugs, jugs, money boxes, plant pots and more. For what it's worth, I am told unicorns are the big thing in the clay-making world at the moment.

Established in 2011 by former art teacher Janet Craig, Hands-on Art's *modus operandi* is to spread the joy of pottery and painting to kids, adults and everyone in between. Education remains Janet's primary pursuit, which is handy, since visitors tend to arrive with zero experience – but after an hour under Janet's wing, they'll not only have something to show for it, they'll have the unforgettable experience of watching their creation go from being a lump of clay, to a fully formed piece of pottery.

A room full of such experiences makes for a great atmosphere. Sure, the setting is nothing special (it's what you get when you cross a cottage industry with a semi-detached house), but on any given day, you'll find the space teeming with have-a-go potters and painters, working to the soundtrack of clinking ceramic and breathing in the wafts of glaze and paints and slowly baking clay. On the first Friday of the month, those of a saucy disposition come for the infamous Pottery & Prosecco evening. You can imagine the kind of things they tend to make.

Spare yourself that gaudy teacup for £10. Get hands-on and come away from Windsor with not only a fresh bit of tat, but the satisfaction of having made it yourself.

Address 42a St Luke's Road, Old Windsor SL4 2QQ, +44 (0)1753 206265, www.hands-onartadventures.co.uk | Getting there Bus 1, 8 or 440 to Toby Carvery; nearby parking at Old Windsor Parish Council Car Park | Hours These vary between term-time and school holidays so check the website for details – booking ahead is essential | Tip Continuing the major theme, across Straight Road from the Toby Carvery you'll spot The Tapestries, a private housing estate that can boast of being one of the finest examples of Arts and Crafts architecture in the county.

36 Havana House
Churchill would blush

At first glance, a cigar shop may seem like an anachronism on a British high street. But you would do Havana House a great disservice to call it that, for this unpretentious store deals in much more than tobacco – it sells aspiration. Of course cigars, fine alcohols and smoking paraphernalia may not seem particularly desirable to some people, but manager Paresh Patel doesn't waste time worrying about 'some people'. He knows that his demographic understands the choiceness of his finely curated wares, sourced from hard-to-reach corners of the world and sold right here in the lavish surroundings of the former Windsor Royal Station.

Mr Patel is quite strict about the fact Havana House is nothing less than a lifestyle brand, and is keen to emphasise how his business extends far beyond the walk-in humidor and ceiling-high liquor cabinets. At his monthly cigar evenings, distinguished guests are invited to partake of his latest acquisitions in decadent surroundings accompanied by on-brand Latin jazz, swing dancing and Cuban cuisine, and you can bet you'll see more than a few velvet smoking jackets. There is even the option to embark on a 'cigar cruise', a journey down the Thames made all the more refined when the taste of a fine Cuban has you imagining yourself island-hopping around the Caribbean.

In accordance with strict British laws, I am not about to advocate that anyone take up smoking. But if you are over 18 and feel so inclined, you might want to pop down to Havana House's second outlet on 44 Thames Street to enjoy a stogie in their sampling lounge. The experts will be more than happy to help you pick a flavour to suit your palate, which you can then enjoy in laid-back fashion surrounded by other like-minded *aficionados*. You're likely to bump into a few Americans, keen to enjoy the rare taste of a Cuban cigar, which are still banned in their home country.

Address Unit 22, Windsor Royal Station, Jubilee Arch, Windsor SL4 1PJ, +44 (0)1753 833334, www.havanahouse.co.uk | Getting there Train to either Windsor & Eton Riverside or Windsor & Eton Central, then a five-minute walk; served by most bus routes | Hours Mon–Sat 10am–6pm, Sun 11am–5pm | Tip Tourists often miss the cut-through to Goswell Hill opposite the front door to the shop. Beneath the arches lies Windsor's nightlife district. My recommendation goes to Fuzzy Bear, which combines cocktails with stand-up comedy for a sensational night out.

37 Hawker Hurricane Monument

The plane that saved Britain

I beg your pardon, why is there a fighter plane whizzing through Alexandra Park? Fret not: this replica of a Hawker Hurricane is just on its way home, heading for 10 Alma Road, the childhood residence of its creator Sir Sydney Camm.

As a young boy, Sir Sydney had a reputation around Windsor as a fervent aerophile. Aged 17, he founded the Windsor Model Aeroplane Club, and the models he didn't fly himself he sold at Herbert's Supply Store on Eton High Street, or better yet, directly to the boys at Eton College, who paid extra to have them winched through their windows in the dead of night.

Eventually, Sir Sydney discovered that model-making was not enough to satisfy his impossibly large appetite and so, in 1923, he joined the Hawker Engineering Company. Within two years, he had risen to the rank of Chief Designer, and in this role he would go on to design 52 types of plane, including the one he is best remembered for: the Hurricane.

Building on his previous design for the Fury, Sir Sydney endowed the Hurricane with a steel-tube structure and low, full-metal wings, making it both agile and durable. At the Battle of Britain in June 1940, the Hurricane showed its mettle by outperforming its rival, the Supermarine Spitfire, to account for 55 per cent of the 2,739 German losses.

Staying with Hawker until 1965, Sir Sydney went went on to design the Typhoon, Tempest, Harrier and, finally, his *magnum opus*, the turbojet-engined Hunter. It remains unknown if he ever achieved satisfaction, but one thing that may give him eternal fulfilment is to know model aeroplane flying remains a popular pastime in Windsor, now in the guise of the Windsor Great Park Flying Association.

Address Barry Avenue, Windsor SL4 5HZ | Getting there Train to Windsor & Eton Central, then a 10-minute walk; bus 7, 8, 71, 191, 702 or 703 to Windsor Boys' School | Tip Walk past the blue plaque on Sir Sydney's childhood home of 10 Alma Road to the Windsor & Royal Borough Museum, which has an exhibition of his life along with a bronze bust sculpted by Ambrose Barker, on loan from the Sir Sydney Camm Commemorative Society.

38 Hawthorn Hill

A hidden treasure in the Berkshire countryside

If you love a good origin myth, you're gonna love the story of Hawthorn Hill.

There was once a pub that sat beneath a hill, on top of which was a lone hawthorn tree. One night, the innkeeper of this pub heard a voice in his dream telling him to go to London Bridge: 'There you will find a great treasure,' said the voice. The innkeeper had never been to London, but the allure of fortune was too great to pass up. The next morning, he hitched his wagon and headed for the city.

When he arrived in London, the innkeeper could find no clue as to where his fortune might be hidden. Just as he was about to give up, a local man came wandering over. 'You lookin' for sumfink?' he asked. 'Yes,' replied the innkeeper, 'I've come in search of a great fortune!'

'You'll find no fortunes 'ere, let me tell ya,' said the man. 'Mind you, I 'eard a voice in me dreams the other night, tellin' me I'd find a great treasure if I dug under an 'awthorn tree on some 'illtop. Good job I'm not as daft as you to go lookin' for it!' You don't say, thought the innkeeper, already packing up his wagon to run home. When he got to the hawthorn tree above his pub, he started digging, and soon stumbled upon a clay pot with a Latin inscription. 'Tsk! Not quite the treasure I was hoping for!' Nonetheless, he put the pot on display above his bar as a memento of his adventure.

A while later, an Oxford scholar popped in for a drink. 'This pot has a strange inscription,' the scholar remarked upon seeing the vessel. '"Beneath where this pot stood, there is another twice as good" – that's what it says in Latin. I wonder what it means?' Hearing this, the innkeeper ran back to the hawthorn tree and dug again. Sure enough, a little deeper, he unearthed another clay pot – except this time, it was full of gold! Thus, the legend of the Hawthorn Hill, from which this idyllic village gets its name, was born.

Address Hawthorn Hill, Bracknell RG42 6HE | **Getting there** By car, follow either the A330 (Ascot Road) or A3095 (Maidenhead Road) until the two roads meet in a three-way junction. Best place for parking is Fernygrove Farm (see the Tip). | **Hours** For Fernygrove Farm: Tue–Sat 9am–3pm | **Tip** Nowadays, Hawthorn Hill is a quiet hamlet of only a few houses, but there is one establishment that brings visitors from near and far: Fernygrove Farm (RG42 6HN). Stop by the café to sample what is perhaps the best bacon in the whole county.

39 Herne's Oak Shakespeare
The heartbroken hunter of Windsor

Travellers, beware! If you are ever caught wandering about Windsor Great Park on a still winter's night, a horned apparition will surely appear before you. This is the spirit of Herne the Hunter – once a noble and virtuous huntsman, now a wayward wraith hell-bent on revenge.

Herne was the most skilled and brave of all of King Richard II's hunters: so skilled, that he attracted the envy of the king's other huntsmen; and so brave that one day while on a hunt, as the king faced certain death at the horns of a frenzied stag, Herne leapt to the king's rescue. Whilst he managed to save the king, Herne gravely injured himself in the process. The distraught king called upon a mysterious wizard named Urswick to save Herne's life – but the jealous hunters had other ideas. They threatened the cowardly Urswick, so that the wizard was forced to make a bargain: he would obey the king and save Herne, but in doing so would strip him of his ability to hunt.

When Herne recovered, he found he could no longer shoot his arrows, and was summarily dismissed by the king. Disgraced and forsaken, Herne took himself deep into the forest and hanged himself from an ancient oak. From then on, it was said that all who passed by this oak would meet a spirit wearing the antlers of a stag, swearing vengeance upon those who had disgraced him in life.

For generations, the residents of Windsor remained so fearful of Herne's Oak that in 1863 it was chopped down. The last surviving vestige of the tree was given to Queen Victoria's woodcarver, William Perry, who fashioned it into a bust of Shakespeare, since the Bard had immortalised Herne in his tale *The Merry Wives of Windsor*. The bust itself is now hidden from view, locked away in the collection of the Windsor & Royal Borough Museum, but some speculate it may return to the gallery soon. Perhaps we should all fear such a day will ever come…

Address Windsor & Royal Borough Museum, 51 High Street, Windsor SL4 1LR, +44 (0)1628 685686, www.windsormuseum.org.uk | Getting there Look for the entrance under the canopy of Windsor Guildhall | Hours Wed–Sun 10am–4pm | Tip The bust is currently in storage, and can only be viewed by appointment. As for Herne's spirit? Perhaps you'll encounter it yourself while traipsing through the Great Park at night.

40 Herschel Monument
Windsor's brightest star

Sir William Herschel came from Hanover to England in 1757 as a journeyman composer, working stints in Newcastle, Durham, Halifax and Bath. But music was never his true calling, and he soon switched professions to become an astronomer. He had a particular interest in studying the planets, but found the rudimentary telescopes of the day to be nowhere near strong enough. Thus, he set about creating his own. He even went so far as to create his own super-sized mirrors, giving his contraptions a whopping 6,450 times magnification.

One night in 1781, while charting the night sky with his sister Caroline, Herschel stumbled upon something he hadn't seen before. This turned out to be none other than Uranus, making it the first planet to be discovered since prehistoric times. Herschel originally dubbed it *Georgium Sidus* – 'the Georgian planet' – which rather endeared him to George III and earned him the title of Royal Astronomer.

Herschel continued his house-hopping journey to Windsor to be closer to his new mate, the king. He moved first to Horton Road, Datchet, then to Clayhall Farm in Old Windsor, and finally Observatory House, Slough, where he lived out the rest of his life. At Observatory House, Herschel built what was then the world's largest and most powerful telescope, with which he looked deeper into space than any human being before him. From Slough, he discovered two new moons of Saturn, while Caroline discovered eight new comets.

In true Slough fashion, Observatory House was demolished in 1963 to make way for an office block. This token monument, designed by Czech sculptor Franta Belsky, now stands alone outside the new building on the aptly-named Herschel Road. A far more fitting memorial is a two-telescope observatory in Eton College, opened in 1983 by Herschel's great-great-granddaughter Caroline and now home to the Herschel Astronomical Society.

Address Observatory House, 25 Windsor Road, Slough SL1 2EL | Getting there Train to either Windsor & Eton Riverside or Windsor & Eton Central, then a 15-minute walk; bus 15, 63 or 68 to Broken Furlong, then a five-minute walk north along the viaduct footpath | Tip If you'd like to pay a visit to William Herschel's grave, he was laid to rest in 1822 in the churchyard of St Laurence's, Slough (SL3 7LS). A stained-glass window in the church also depicts the cosmos as it was mapped by Herschel.

41 History on Wheels
More fun than you could shake a gear stick at

History on Wheels could be called a museum, but really it is an animated memorial to one of Windsor's most talented collectors. The man behind it all, Tony Oliver, devoted his life to finding and restoring vintage automobiles and World War II paraphernalia. Along the way, he acquired so many rare and fascinating items, including a mint-condition Citroen B-14 Paris taxi and General McArthur's 1941 Cadillac (a car he literally wrote the book on), that the only logical next step was to open this museum in 1978.

Words can hardly do the experience justice, but here goes nothing: as you enter the main hall, an animatronic sergeant waves hello. Postman Pat smiles from behind the wheel of a red Morris 5 CWT. Walk past the arcade game *Run Adolf Run* (5p a play), where the aim is to shoot out Hitler's teeth with a pistol, and check out the M4 Sherman tank that starred in the 1967 film *The Dirty Dozen*. Stop at the NAAFI tuck shop, where an eerily attractive, robotic matron sells cigarettes. Take a nap in the Anderson air raid shelter (don't mind the baby in the gas mask), then pop next door to listen to the story of Tony's extraordinary life in the cinema, where even the fittings – rescued from an Art Deco cinema in Nazi-occupied Jersey – add to his legend. If this all sounds a bit absurd, know that I have barely scratched the surface.

Tony's tastes were diverse to say the least, and as such his museum is sprawling. Just when you think you've reached the end, you find the room where he displayed his Enfield motorcycles and vintage firefighting equipment next to his wife Vera's collection of Charles and Diana porcelain. What is most beautiful is not any of the cars or trinkets, but the love with which Tony's son Peter continues to run his late father's museum. Without funding, it can only afford to open a few days a year, but you should make sure you're here when it does.

Address Longclose House, Common Road, Eton Wick SL4 6QY, +44 (0)1753 833833, www.historyonwheels.co.uk | Getting there Bus 15, 63 or 68 to The Walk/Greyhound Public House, then a 15-minute walk | Hours Mostly Sundays and Bank Holidays 10am – 4 or 5pm, but see website for upcoming dates and times | Tip Stop by The Greyhound on your way back for a bite to eat and a game in their indoor skittle alley. Just look for the pub with the crocodile on the roof.

42 Holy Trinity Garrison Church

Salvation for Windsor's seedy soldiers

Windsor has been a garrison town since its earliest days, when William the Conqueror's Norman soldiers were posted here to defend the first iteration of Windsor Castle. Troops would come and go over the following centuries until the town added its first permanent barracks in 1800 to train soldiers for the war against France; one of these cantonments remains today as the Victoria Barracks.

Being a garrison town meant that, at any given time, up to 30 per cent of Windsor's population would be young men, and you can imagine the kind of problems this caused. Drunkenness, outbreaks of smallpox, the harassment of young women and the solicitation of prostitutes were all rife, according to local newspapers. The overarching feeling around town was that the soldiers were not only lawless, but Godless, and that something would have to be done about it if Windsor was to achieve harmony between civvies and squaddies.

The town thus decided to pool together and provide a garrison church for the soldiers. Contributions were drawn from all over, with the lion's share coming from Queen Victoria. Edward Blore, best known for his work on Buckingham Palace, was chosen as the architect, and while his design was panned for being a bit plain, the church opened in 1844 to great success.

It continues to be used today in the unique role of both a parish church and a garrison church. Whatever your opinion about how it looks from the outside, you'll find the interior quite striking indeed. Barely an inch of wall remains that doesn't bear a touching tribute to a fallen comrade, while two standards from the Battle of Waterloo hang over the pews. Beside the altar rests the Falklands Cross, salvaged from a makeshift grave in the South Atlantic to commemorate the lives lost in the sinking of the HMS *Sir Galahad*.

Address Trinity Place, Windsor SL4 3AX, +44 (0)1753 862776, www.windsorchurches.org.uk/holy-trinity-church | Getting there Train to either Windsor & Eton Central or Windsor & Eton Riverside, then a 10-minute walk; bus 1, W1, 2, 8, 9, 10, 16, 600, 702 or 703 | Hours Wed–Fri 9.30–11.30am, sometimes open on Saturdays | Tip Continue your church-walking tour to Alma Road, where you'll find the splendid Windsor Catholic Church of St Edward and St Mark, opened 1868 and designed by architect Charles Alban Buckler.

43 A Hoppy Place
Berkshire's craft beer crucible

Many people in Windsor and Maidenhead remark that the borough is starting to feel like an exclave of Hackney. Not that that's necessarily a bad thing. This cultural shift is bringing radical independents back to the fore, creating a hyper-local environment where new tastes and fresh perspectives thrive. A Hoppy Place, which is actually two hoppy places – one in Windsor, one in Maidenhead – is at the forefront of the two towns' changing identities, offering the kind of hipster hangout the towns' rapidly growing millennial contingents have been craving.

Having said that, the idea was drawn not from London, but from America. Husband-and-wife co-founders Dave and Naomi Hayward discovered the craft beer revolution engulfing California and knew right away that Windsor needed the same sort of insurrection. Their first bottle shop opened its doors in Windsor in 2019, just in time for the pandemic. Not that this slowed them down – by 2021, they were already SIBA UK Craft Beer Retailer of the Year, and a household name for microbrew zealots around town. The Maidenhead branch followed in June 2022, and the business has recently expanded again, this time by opening its own brewery, Indie Rabble.

It's a glorious remedy to the overflowing tranche of pubs across the borough that use their 'historic' status to get away with serving the same five brands of lager. Let them rest on their laurels – meanwhile, the punks are holed up here, casually carving out a new history. Now we are in our plywood wall phase, our steel barstool years, our brewed-in-an-attic chapter. And jolly good to be here too. As Berkshire's brewing heritage comes roaring back, with breweries springing up in exotic places like Reading, Finchampstead, White Waltham, and of course Windsor, A Hoppy Place is the one carrying the standard into battle. Pay a visit, and discover your hoppy place.

Address Windsor: 11 St Leonards Road, Windsor SL4 3BN; Maidenhead: Unit C, Trinity Place, Park Street, Maidenhead SL6 1TJ, www.ahoppyplace.co.uk | Getting there Windsor: Train to either Windsor & Eton Central or Windsor & Eton Riverside; Maidenhead: Train to Maidenhead (Elizabeth Line) | Hours Windsor: Tue 3–9pm, Wed noon–9pm, Thu noon–10pm, Fri & Sat noon–10.30pm, Sun noon–8pm; Maidenhead: Tue & Wed noon–9pm, Thu noon–10pm, Fri & Sat noon–11pm, Sun noon–8pm | Tip Two Flints Brewery, which can be found next door to Indie Rabble (The Arches, SL4 1QZ), marks the start of what is quickly becoming known as the Windsor Beer Mile.

44 Irish Guard Statue

A memorial to modern soldiers

Despite being within living memory, Britain has been uncomfortably quiet when it comes to memorialising the 457 military personnel who lost their lives in the Iraq and Afghanistan wars. National and local acts of remembrance still take a very world war-led point of view, despite these conflicts being long gone. I won't speculate as to why that might be the case, but what I will say is that Windsor is very fortunate to be one of the few places in the country to have a unique monument to those recent conflicts in the form of this statue by Mark 'Jacko' Jackson.

The anonymous paratrooper was the first of his kind in the UK to be sculpted in modern combat fatigues and Osprey body armour. He is, literally, battle-hardened: his constitution is of bronze salvaged from the ruins of Iraq, while the rubble beneath his feet is similarly recovered from Afghanistan. He stands pensive and analytical, yet athletic in stature – a soldier, yes, but also a human being. It is as if we have caught him in a moment of ill discipline – he grips his SA 80 by the stock in one hand, while his helmet hangs by his other side – but that would only be true if we assume he is heading into, rather than away from, a battle.

Sculptor Mark Jackson was quite familiar with his subject matter, being the son of General Sir Mike Jackson, and having served as a paratrooper himself until an injury forced his early retirement. He claims that his piece is purposely ambiguous as if to represent any British paratrooper from the last 70 years. Yet, at the unveiling in 2011, it was hard not to draw a connection to local serviceman Major Matthew Collins, who had tragically lost his life in Afghanistan just a few months before.

The Irish Guard remains a bittersweet reminder: bitter, because of that dreadful conflict; sweet, for the memory of the valiant servicemen and women who faced it head-on.

Address On the corner of High Street and St Alban's Street, Windsor SL4 1PF | Getting there Train to either Windsor & Eton Central or Windsor & Eton Riverside, then a five-minute walk; served by most bus routes | Tip Behind the statue you'll no doubt spot the 'Ancient Well'. How someone arrived at the conclusion there is a well here, I don't know – it was never included on any old maps. Maybe it's actually part of a secret tunnel leading from the barracks to the castle…

45 The Italian Shop
Maidenhead's 'Little Italy'

The Italian contribution to Berkshire is easy to overlook but hard to dismiss. A wave of migration in the 1960s brought with it new fashions, new food, and a workforce that was ready to propel local businesses to the forefront of global industry. Nowhere was this more apparent than in the Mars chocolate factory in Slough, which recruited fresh-faced Italians in their droves.

One couple swept to British shores around this time were Carmelo and Assunta Sardo. Being the entrepreneurial types, their destination was not the factory, but rather Slough Market. Recognising both the needs of expat Italians, who craved the authentic foods of their home country, and also the appetites of local people, who were becoming accustomed to these rich flavours themselves, they established their own stall specialising in imported produce – fresh pastas, succulent meats, delicate wines, and more than a few specialist items from their own native Sicily.

From their humble van, the business has grown and grown, first to a corner shop in Maidenhead, then into its own supermarket-sized unit in 2012. Carmelo has since sadly passed away, but the mantle has been taken up by his grandson Massimo, who leads a team still mostly hand-picked from the Sardo family. Even today, Assunta can be found working hard behind the scenes, smushing tomatoes to make the store's own sauces.

Despite being established in England since 1968, the shop still brims with the frenetic energy of Italy. The aisles overflow with packets of pasta, packs of mozzarella fall out of fridges, boxes of Panettone swing from the ceilings, and you can read a copy of Italian newspaper *La Notizia* as you wait in the mile-long queue for the deli. Don't be afraid to ask the staff for help – they may poke fun at each other in rapid-fire Sicilian, but their English is so polite and impeccable, you'd think you were in Italian Harrods.

Address Jubilee House, Denmark Street, Maidenhead SL6 7BN, +44 (0)1628 770110, www.italiancont.co.uk | Getting there Train to Maidenhead (Elizabeth Line), then a 20-minute walk; bus 9 or 155 to Craufurd Rise Railway Bridge, or 37 to Australia Avenue, then a five-minute walk; free parking on site | Hours Tue–Sat 11am–7pm | Tip If you are heading back to Windsor, another Italian destination you must try is Don Beni (42 High Street, Eton SL4 6BD; www.don-beni-restaurant.co.uk). Since 1993, it has been a Berkshire institution, offering an authentic taste of Italy at an affordable price.

46 John F. Kennedy Memorial

A small corner of America in Runnymede

The assassination of John F. Kennedy on 22 November, 1963 came as a shock to the British political elite. Under Kennedy, the UK and the USA had been inching closer to their professed 'special relationship'. Something had to be done to reiterate Britain's support for America, and so the idea for a national memorial received quick, cross-party approval. As a demonstration of intention, Prime Minister Alec Douglas-Home attached a price tag of £1 million to the monument, with Sir James Harman, Lord Mayor of London, tasked with raising the funds.

There was one problem, which was that the British people were ambivalent towards this show of political gushiness. Kennedy had been a schismatic figure in Britain, both because of his silver-spoon heritage and his stuttering approach to the civil rights movement. The fundraising drive was so slow moving that it outlasted Douglas-Home's tenure, forcing his successor Harold Wilson to finish the project with state funds. It was finally completed and unveiled by Queen Elizabeth II in 1965.

The site is jam-packed with on-the-nose symbolism. The choice of Runnymede as the location was intended to represent the democratic legacy that binds Britain and America; a hawthorn tree in the vicinity nods to Kennedy's Catholic faith, while an American scarlet oak blooms in November, the month of his death; beneath the Seats of Contemplation, a ha-ha was dug to illustrate that no border exists between British and American soil – indeed, the whole acre of land was given to the United States.

Far from strengthening relations, the monument actually became a target for anti-Vietnam War protestors, and was damaged by a bomb attack in 1968. There is at least one part that remains popular: the Kennedy Scholarship, which offers British post-grads the chance to study in America, was established as a living supplement to the memorial.

THIS ACRE OF ENGLISH GROUND WAS GIVEN
TO THE UNITED STATES OF AMERICA BY
THE PEOPLE OF BRITAIN IN MEMORY OF
JOHN F KENNEDY
PRESIDENT OF THE UNITED STATES 1961-63
DIED BY AN ASSASSIN'S HAND 22 NOVEMBER 1963
LET EVERY NATION KNOW WHETHER IT WISHES US WELL OR ILL
THAT WE SHALL PAY ANY PRICE BEAR ANY BURDEN MEET ANY HARDSHIP
SUPPORT ANY FRIEND OR OPPOSE ANY FOE IN ORDER TO ASSURE
THE SURVIVAL AND SUCCESS OF LIBERTY

Address Windsor Road, Englefield Green TW20 0YU, www.kennedytrust.org.uk/
runnymede | Getting there Parking is available at Runnymede Memorials Car Park
(SL4 2JL) and Runnymede Riverside Car Park (SL4 2JN), both accessed via the A308 |
Tip The USA's connection to Runnymede actually started in 1957, when the American
Bar Association funded the creation of the nearby Magna Carta Memorial, a Neo-classical
rotunda designed by Sir Edward Maufe.

47 Jubilee River Walk
What a relief

The Thames giveth, the Thames taketh away. Life by the river affords many advantages, but it also brings the risk of flooding. The floods at Windsor featured regularly in *The Illustrated London News* throughout the 1800s – one artist's impression from 1875 showed gondolas gliding down Windsor's totally inundated streets.

In 1995, the town decided that enough was enough. It was time to try something drastic. The Thames Flood Alleviation Scheme was put in motion, with the plan to create a hydraulic channel taking excess water from the Thames at Maidenhead and returning it at Datchet. It would end up costing a cool £110 million and took seven years to complete, arriving just in time for Queen Elizabeth II's Golden Jubilee, hence the name. The Jubilee River was an instant success, and Windsor has never seen flooding again since.

LOL, just kidding. By January 2003, the river had already failed in its design as Windsor saw its worst flood since 1947. Datchet, being on the receiving end of the torrent's outlet, got hit twice as hard. Another £5 million was added to the bill to fund the repairs. It worked, and everyone lived happily ever after.

LOL, just kidding. Windsor flooded again in 2014, with Datchet once again taking the lion's share. *Sigh.* Will it ever end? Who knows, but let's not let it get us down. Let's instead be glad the engineers were kind enough to install a fantastic footpath along the riverside.

And what a path! From Eton, you skirt around the outside of the playing fields, serenaded by an orchestra of cornflowers. From here, the space opens up to meadows of buttercups and daisies. Step up the Allotments Footbridge to see the lily pads floating near the weir, enjoy a spot of trainspotting on Chalvey Rail Bridge, and for God's sake bring a bike – National Route 61 runs along the path and is the best way to see Windsor's greatest hubris.

Address The path is 7.2 miles long and runs from Maidenhead to Eton and Slough | **Getting there** Free parking at Marsh Lane (Taplow SL6 0EB) and Jubilee River Riverside Centre, Slough Road (Slough SL1 2BP); pay & display parking at Boulter's Lock Car Park, Lower Cookham Rd (Maidenhead SL6 8JN) | **Tip** Windsor's worst floods occurred in 1774, 1894 and 1947. A flood level marker by Barnes Pool in Eton shows how high the torrents reached during those years.

48 Julian Bettney Fine Art

Step inside the mind of a genius

'This one,' Julian begins, pointing towards a canvas of a painted blue sky with a single white cloud and a silver, Concorde-shaped entity lurking in the vapour wisps, 'is a UFO that visited me in my back garden a few weeks ago.' The word 'eclectic' doesn't do Julian Bettney's studio justice. The jury's out on whether to even call it a studio. All at once, it is an architectural salvage shop, a museum, a painting restoration workshop and a picture framer's, the latter being Julian's busiest commercial enterprise. You can even come to Julian to purchase property in Ibiza, if you so wish.

Really, the space is the embodiment of the man himself, a living representation of what goes on in an artist's head – utter chaos that falls together, somehow, to form a breathtaking aesthetic. Whatever you come here for, two things are guaranteed: first, that before you know it, Julian will lock you into a conversation probing the nature of the universe until you arrive at the conclusion you are two souls germinated from the same cosmic seed; and second, that you will be given the grand tour of Julian's workshop, a romantic mess of unused lengths of picture frame and shards of glass repurposed as paint palettes and scattered wantonly across every inch of his desk. This room was also once his bedroom, but don't worry – he's since moved to a very swish part of West Windsor.

Julian's brilliance shines out of every corner. Note the paint splatters on the front windowsill, where he takes his canvases to work on sunny days. Clock the fresco on the ceiling of the porch (Michelangelo eat your heart out). The doormat is made of vintage iron plaques, obviously. Whir around the gallery to see Julian's latest brainwaves on his antique easels, or his collection of paintings by Charles Gerrard. You'll soon realise why this space has been admired throughout its 31 years by the likes of Madonna, Prince Edward, Chris Martin and, apparently, many extraterrestrials.

Address The Old Bank, The Green, Datchet SL3 9JH, +44 (0)7770 762468, www.facebook.com/JulianBettneyFineArt | **Getting there** Train to Datchet | **Hours** Daily (mostly) 3 – 7pm | **Tip** If Julian's not in when you arrive, it's probably because he's popped over the road to Nibbles café. Go and meet him there, and stop for a spot of afternoon tea while you're at it.

49 The Jurors

Twelve angry men?

Twelve empty chairs sit around an invisible table, begging many questions. Are they set up for a dinner party? A business meeting? A summit? Perhaps we're asking the wrong questions. Perhaps these chairs have no intrinsic meaning. Perhaps meaning can only be bestowed upon them by the actions of the persons seated there. If you've come to Runnymede with 11 friends, why not each take a pew and see what happens next. Will you have an amiable chat, an intellectual discussion, a heated debate? Will you break bread and share happy memories, or will you be overcome by the fury of war and leap across the void at your friend opposite?

You are in control of your own destiny as you sit at *The Jurors*, a contemplative installation by titanic sculptor Hew Locke. I could tell you about the background to this piece – commissioned by the National Trust and Surrey County Council to mark the 800th year of Magna Carta, yadda yadda, blah blah – but it's not the story of how they came to be in Runnymede that makes them significant. Rather, it's the heavy symbolism that each bronze chair carries.

Law, freedom, human rights, justice – these are but a few of the overarching themes, represented by a series of friezes cast upon both sides of the 12 chair backs. Collectively, they show both the good and bad sides of the democratic legacy. From the Ancient Egyptian scales of justice, to the Confucian values of *Ren, Li* and *Yi,* to the UN's Rights of the Child on the side of the good; to an oil tanker run aground, a boat weighed down by refugees, and the slave ship Zong, scene of a brutal massacre, on the side of the bad.

Don't be disheartened, for there is light to be found in the darkness: the portraits of freedom fighters such as suffragette Lilian Lenton and Indian lawyer Cornelia Sorabji inspire us to choose the side of the good, while at the head of the table, Nelson Mandela's prison cell sits empty, the key within an arm's reach of the bars.

Address Windsor Road, Englefield Green TW20 0YU | Getting there Parking is available at Runnymede Memorials Car Park (SL4 2JL) and Runnymede Riverside Car Park (SL4 2JN), both accessed via the A308 | Tip Fans of Sir Edwin Lutyens will inevitably turn their attention to his gatehouses at the eastern and western entrances to Runnymede. But did you know he also designed the nearby Egham Roundabout?

50 King John's Palace

A home fit for England's worst king

Well, someone clearly had a sense of humour. Not to disappoint you if you've come to Colnbrook expecting a literal palace, but what we have before us is anything but.

Which isn't to say it's not quite astonishing. The oldest residence in Colnbrook (and that's saying something), King John's Palace is a distinguished example of a well-lived-in Tudor house that retains all of its rickety crookedness, from its rendered walls made from layers of limewash, to the casement windows that look as if they'd cause a few problems in the winter.

If you can steal a glance through these windows – being mindful of the residents' privacy – you'll note the interiors to be just as authentically period, with teeny-tiny doors and head-bumpingly low ceilings. The front façade looks a bit unloved of late (best to ignore the dilapidated pub next door), but your eyes will probably bypass these walls and settle instead on the enormous elliptical archway leading to the eaves, which hints at the building's original use as a coaching inn.

While this building has 'only' been around since roughly 1600, its name is a reference to 'Bad' King John I, who is alleged to have stayed in a previous iteration of this house on his way from Windsor to Runnymede to sign Magna Carta. The sheer normalcy of the site is symbolic of the king's almighty humbling, and the irony implicit in the name may have been the work of some smug baron.

From a coaching inn, to a school, to a residential estate, this building has seen its fair share of history. One moment in particular has ramifications for your fruit bowl, for in a field just down the road from here Richard Cox cultivated the first Cox Orange Pippin apple in 1825. The plot behind King John's Palace is still used for farming today – this time, however, it is alpacas rather than apples that are reared in this quirky corner of Colnbrook.

Address 1–6 Park Street, Colnbrook SL3 0HS | Getting there Bus 81, 305 or 703 to The Star & Garter | Hours Viewable from the outside only | Tip Further along Bath Road is Station Cottage (SL3 0NJ). From 1884 to 1965, this was Colnbrook's railway station, on the now closed line between West Drayton and Staines West. Part of the tracks and railway infrastructure can still be seen alongside this cottage today.

51 Kingsmead Quarry Finds

Windsor's first housing estate

Around 4,000 B.C., the people of south-east England decided they'd had enough of being hunter-gatherers and started to settle on small farmsteads. These plucky communities tended to situate themselves on fertile plains close to rivers, where all the vital elements of life could be found in abundance. The Thames Basin made the ideal breeding ground for some of England's first significant societies.

One of the most impressive communities to arise in this era was at the site of what is now Kingsmead Quarry. From 2003 to 2012, a meticulous investigation by Wessex Archaeology revealed evidence of a civilisation here dating as far back as 10,000 B.C. With waterholes for cattle and plots for roundhouses, this prehistoric community was clearly not only large, it was technologically adept. They were around for a while, too, as the continuity of finds suggests they were still going strong well into the Roman era.

One discovery made at the site is unique to Britain: the body of an adult woman, buried over 4,300 years ago, clutching a beaker vessel and wearing an ornate necklace of gold and amber beads. The amber may have been sourced from as far away as the Baltics, suggesting this woman – probably the head of a local tribe – oversaw a shipping route extending all the way to Eastern Europe. Further evidence of this vast trade network is provided by a decorative pin, seemingly sourced from the Picardy region of France. Just how did these continental artefacts find their way into the hands of villagers in prehistoric Horton?

It is not an exaggeration to say that Kingsmead Quarry is one of the most important archaeological sites in Britain, a window into life going as far back as the Ice Age. A sample of the finds can be found tucked away in the corner of the Windsor & Royal Borough Museum, collectively painting an extraordinary picture of life in pre-historic Britain.

Address Windsor & Royal Borough Museum, 51 High Street, Windsor SL4 1LR, +44 (0)1628 685686, www.windsormuseum.org.uk | Getting there Train to Windsor & Eton Central, then a five-minute walk; look for the entrance under the canopy of Windsor Guildhall | Hours Wed – Sun 10am – 4pm | Tip Armchair archaeologists will be disappointed by Windsor, where much of the ancient landscape is private and therefore inaccessible. But in nearby Bracknell, it's the other way around. Check out Bill Hill (RG12 7AZ), a prehistoric bowl barrow converted into a delightful woodland walk.

52 Lamppost 007
The name's Post. Lamp Post.

Born in 1908 to a nouveau-riche family, Ian Lancaster Fleming was a badly behaved, dour and academically underperforming boy. Eton educations ran in the family, and it was Fleming's mother's hope that this would help to straighten her son out.

When he arrived at Eton College, Fleming was sorted into The Timbralls dormitory, under the sadistic jurisdiction of housemaster Sam Slater, from whom Fleming was a regular recipient of canings. While this imbued him with an abhorrence of authority, it did nothing to raise his grades. Where Fleming did excel, however, was on the sports field – he was the first boy to be named *Victor Ludorum* (champion sportsman) in two consecutive years.

Another avenue he excelled in was writing. Encouraged by his friend and fellow litterateur Ivar Bryce, Fleming produced his first short story, a warped tale of domestic vengeance, for the school magazine *The Wyvern*. Bryce was also known to lead Fleming astray, and the pair would often ride out on clandestine motorcycle journeys. On one excursion, Fleming claimed to have lost his virginity on the floor of a Windsor cinema.

This and other scenes from Fleming's life at Eton inspired the adventures of a character later to become a household name: secret agent James Bond. Like Fleming, Bond was a loner, a hedonist and a stoic. And, like Fleming, Bond showed disdain for authority and intellectualism, preferring instead to play games and chase pretty girls.

When it came to naming his character, Fleming appropriated the name James Bond from – of all people – an American ornithologist. As for the infamous codename '007', local legend posits Fleming took the number from this lamppost located just up the road from his dorm room at The Timbralls. Whether or not the rumour is true (it is one of dozens of such theories), this otherwise inconspicuous pole has become something of a shrine for Bond fans.

Address Slough Road, Windsor SL4 6DU | **Getting there** Train to Windsor & Eton Riverside or Windsor & Eton Central, then a 15-minute walk; bus 15, 63 or 68 to Eton College, then head north for five minutes on Slough Road. Look for the lamppost on the north side of the road. | **Tip** Another must-see Bond destination is in the north of Slough. Stoke Park Golf Club (www.stokepark.com) is where James Bond teed off against his nemesis Goldfinger in the 1964 film.

53 Langham Pond

A hidden habitat in Runnymede

When you think you've finished your walk around the meadows of Runnymede, keep walking. Past the Magna Carta Memorial, past Writ in Water (see ch. 109), all the way to the inconspicuous kissing gate on the south-western edge of the fields. Pass through, then carefully traverse the gangplanks across the marshy pits. Once your feet arrive back on solid earth, you'll discover an animated glade where England's ecological splendour bursts to life like nowhere else.

GCSE geography students will easily identify Langham Pond as an ox-bow lake formed from a long-gone meander of the River Thames. Now isolated and no longer flowing, the stagnant waters may appear to the untrained eye almost like a swamp. But to entomologists and botanists – and the organisms they study – this ancient body of water is the quintessential cradle of civilisation.

The whole plot is a roll call of plant and insect life, much of which is so rare as to warrant special protection by the pond's guardians, the National Trust. The abundant supply of common flies buzzing about the lily pads include among their ranks *cerodontha ornata*, a species unique to this corner of Britain, and a rare feast for the herons, little grebes, water rails, and all three species of British woodpecker who stalk them from the wild rhododendrons across the banks.

Meanwhile, within the pond are no fewer than four species of British duckweed, along with a staggering diversity of flora and fauna that won't be found in this assortment anywhere else. Eyes peeled, then, for the whorled water-milfoil, orange foxtail grass, greater water parsnip, rushes (both flowering and round-fruited), arrowhead, fine-leaved water-dropwort, slender tufted sedge and the über-rare frog-bit smut, to name but a few. Don't worry if those names go right over your head – the oil painting-esque vista is bound to impress you nevertheless.

Address Egham TW20 0LB | Getting there Only accessible by foot. Walk south from Runnymede Memorial Car Park to the gate. Or, cross the A308 (Windsor Road) from Runnymede Pleasure Ground and head west. What3words: sunk.mount.help | Tip Continue south along the Ramblers' Route to reach Egham. As a student town, it's rich with great pubs and cafés, but one of particular note is the 16th-century Red Lion at 52 High Street.

54 The Last Supper

Da Vinci's been real quiet since this dropped

The Church of St John the Baptist is to Windsor what St Paul's Cathedral is to London. Sure, it may not compare in the magnitude department, but it has nonetheless acted as the town's focal point since ancient times. It is as vital to the people of Windsor as the letter 'W'.

There are at least a dozen reasons to recommend this church: there's the building itself, built in 1822 by architect Charles Hollis on the site of the previous church, which was probably as old as the town itself; there's the interior walls, a rogue's gallery of plaques commemorating notable people from Windsor's past, many of which were salvaged from the previous building; there's the splendid chancel and apse, added in 1870 by Samuel Sanders Teulon with show-stopping mosaics by Italian glassmith Antonio Salviati; and don't miss the Royal Pews, brought from St George's Chapel by King George III's daughter Augusta.

But the centrepiece is undoubtedly *The Last Supper*, the work of German great Francis de Cleyn, whom King James I imported from the continent to be his personal painter. With its hyperactive *mise en scène*, in which the artist deftly depicts each of the disciples in the various stages of grief, it is enough to give Leonard da Vinci a run for his money. Originally hung in St George's Chapel, the piece fortuitously survived the Civil War with nothing more than a scratch, and was subsequently given to the church and people of Windsor by George III in 1788.

Despite its size, it can be rather easy to miss (not least because of how distracting the church's other treasures can be) – it's located above the balconies on the west wall. Even from a distance, the incredible attention to detail speaks for itself, but if you'd like a more in-depth description, the church has positioned plenty of literature around to guide you through the piece and its history.

Address Windsor Parish Church of St John the Baptist, High Street, Windsor SL4 1LT, +44 (0)1753 862776, www.windsorchurches.org.uk/windsor-parish-church-of-st-john-the-baptist | Getting there Train to either Windsor & Eton Central or Windsor & Eton Riverside, then a five minute walk; served by most bus routes | Hours Daily 9am–5pm | Tip One of the memorials to keep an eye out for in the church is that of Richard Galis, the ignominious landlord of The Harte & Garter who became the central villain in the tale of the Witches of Windsor.

55 — The Limes

A refuge for the women of Windsor

Named after the citrus trees that once graced the garden, this half-timbered cottage is quite a contrast to the surrounding modern houses. Indeed, its ubiquitous constitution betrays the house's rich history, with some parts dating to the 15th century. But it is not the building itself that is significant, rather the life of its most notable tenant – I mean that literally, for her name was Mariquita Tennant.

Born Mariquita Eroles in Barcelona in 1811, Tennant's early life was troubled to say the least. Her father chose the wrong side in the Peninsula War and fled with his family to London in 1823, where Mariquita married her first husband David Reid in 1833. However, Reid died the same year in Florence. Tennant remarried in 1838, this time to Anglican pastor Robert Tennant, but Florence clearly had it in for Mariquita, for Robert also died there in 1842.

While working with four-times Prime Minister William Gladstone to publish her late husband's sermons, Tennant moved to this cottage in Clewer. Here, in 1849, she took a role in charity by opening up her home to care for local women who had been victims of rape and abuse (Tennant called them her 'Magdalens'). She soon found herself caring for 12 such girls, who were stretching her resources thin; thankfully, Gladstone offered to help by purchasing a shelter on Hatch Lane, which became known as the Clewer House of Mercy. The building was soon so full that Tennant employed the women in a laundry business, but running this organisation took a toll on her health. She retired in 1851, leaving the house in the care of the Community of St John the Baptist.

Tennant lived on Claremont Road until her death in 1860, but continued to keep an eye out for her Magdalens as they grew up in Windsor. She was laid to rest in St Andrew's Church (see ch. 77) overlooking the house that cemented her legacy as Windsor's Mother Superior.

Address The Limes, Mill Lane, Windsor SL4 5JE | Getting there Train to Windsor & Eton Central, then a 15-minute walk, or to Windsor & Eton Riverside and a 20-minute walk; bus 2, 8 or 703 to Windsor Boys' School | Hours Viewable from the outside only | Tip Also on Mill Road is Old Mill House. Sir Michael Caine lived here in the 1960s and later sold the property to Jimmy Page, whose Led Zeppelin bandmate John Bonham sadly met his end here. You too can join its roster of famous residents by renting the house on Airbnb.

56 Liquid Leisure

Ridin' some waves in Windsor

It has the largest inhabited castle in the world, and the largest number of veteran oaks in Britain, but did you know Windsor also has the largest wakeboarding park in Europe? It all started with a small town called London, and its insatiable thirst for water. To hydrate the growing populace, tracts of land around Wraysbury were transformed into massive reservoirs throughout the 20th century. The largest, the King George VI Reservoir, was so big it was alleged to have contained a fake Clapham Junction, to confuse German bombers during World War II.

Liquid Leisure's freshwater lake sits within this swathe of reservoirs, but never seems to have been used as one itself. That suited the business' founder, Stuart Marston – coming home from 24 British and European watersports championship wins, he took out a lease on this unused body of water and set about building his watersports empire.

The road to opening day was long, but given the magnitude of Marston's vision, it had to be. The scale is laid bare before us today: a five-tower cable spins waterskiers and wakeboarders at breakneck speeds over jumps and obstacles; speedboats hurtle about pulling banana boats and ringos in their wake; and if open swimming is more your bag, well then, jump right in. Everything is world championship calibre, and sure enough Liquid Leisure has hosted several prestigious competitions since opening in 2017. Away from watersports, you've also got the UK's biggest inflatable aqua park, with assault courses and climbing frames that make a splash with all ages. And if you don't fancy getting in the water? No problem – grab a drink from the poolside bar, catch a tan on the beach, then pitch a tent and camp overnight (would it be clichéd to call Liquid Leisure 'everything under the Sun?').

Let London drink tap water – Windsor has found a hundred other uses for their beloved H_2O.

Address Horton Road, Datchet SL3 9HY, +44 (0)1753 542500,
www.windsor.liquidleisure.com | Getting there Train to Sunnymeads, then a 10-minute
walk to the entrance on Horton Road | Hours Daily noon–8pm | Tip If sailing is more
your cup of tea, head to the adjacent Queen Mother Reservoir where the Datchet Water
Sailing Club practises with dinghies, catamarans, windsurfers and paddleboards. Booking
ahead essential – see www.dwsc.co.uk.

57 Loading Bay Café

Load up on vegan goodness

It's Saturday morning and you fancy brunch. What do you do? Well, you could head to a generic chain café on Peascod Street and compete with crowds of tourists and mimosa-fuelled hen dos for a table. Or, you could venture into Windsor's Vansittart industrial estate and look for the plywood kiosk behind the steel roller shutters, where a breeze of freshly brewed coffee is carried by the romping bomp-bomp-bomp of techno music. If the second option sounds more your sort of thing, park your bum in the Loading Bay Café.

This trendy den is one more in a series of enterprises started by local business 4Motion CIC, founded by performing artist Dean Soden and dancer Elaine Macey. After circling the globe delivering groundbreaking wellbeing programmes, the natural next step was to expand into the food and beverage sector with the intention to tackle loneliness through community building, and to steer people towards sustainable eating. And where better to do this than in the loading bay beneath their studio? Badda bing, badda boom, and the café opened in 2018 to great aplomb.

Every detail harks back to the company ethos. The furniture is all upcycled industrial equipment – cable drums for coffee tables, plastic crates for stools. The menu is locally sourced and 100 per cent plant-based – the only café in town that can boast such credentials. And, like the plants they cook with, the business is an organic entity that grows and grows, nourished by good ideas and positive vibes. That's why on any given day you might encounter a pop-up gemstone store, a stage in the car park giving a platform to local bands, or an exhibition of local artists' works. For something a bit more substantial and intimate, there's even an evening supper club.

No offence to the chain cafés, but all the plastic packets of ham and cheese toasties in the world couldn't hold a candle to this.

Address Kardleton House, Vansittart Estate, Windsor SL4 1SE, www.4motioncic.com/loading-bay-cafe-windsor | **Getting there** Train to Windsor & Eton Central, then a five-minute walk or Windsor & Eton Riverside Station and a 10-minute walk; bus 8 or 703 to Arthur Road | **Hours** Thu & Fri 9am–1.30pm, Sat 9am–2pm, also monthly events, so check the website | **Tip** While walking off your brunch, pop one road over to Duke Street and look for the alleyway between numbers 25 and 27. This will lead you to Gardner Cottages Community Green, a shared garden where locals gather *en masse* in the summer.

58 The Loch & the Tyne

Sustainably luxurious food and lodgings

Trip, fall, and you're likely to land in a plate of good nosh any-where in Windsor. But take a running jump into the bucolic countryside and you may have the good fortune to crash head-long into a plate served by Adam Handling's team at The Loch & the Tyne. The bonnie Scot has curated a menu that brings the fin-est tastes from all corners of the British Isles to one of his newest and most refined enterprises, brought to life by co-chef proprietors Jonny McNeil of St Andrews and Steven Kerr of Newcastle (hence the 'Loch' and the 'Tyne'). From Sunday roasts to fish and chips, and the veggie-friendly mushroom wellington, plus a six-course tasting menu featuring a beautiful, buttery lamb rump, and the absolutely must-try King's Trifle whipped up in honour of Charles III, this is British cuisine reimagined with artful tenacity.

And then there is the setting itself. What was once a rickety roadside pub has been sympathetically regenerated into a vision of eco-friendly hospitality, with an eye on becoming Britain's most sustainable gastropub. The décor is all tastefully upcycled, and the hot water bottle covers were knitted by Adam's mum. Look for the kitchen team foraging in the adjacent countryside, or plucking ingre-dients from the vegetable plot in the beer garden, which is in turn fed by compost from the kitchen and recycled water from the bath-rooms – everything works in a harmonious cycle, adding a feel-good factor to the already infectious charm.

If you're not in the mood for a full dinner, come instead for a cheerful pub sesh. The whisky line-up offers as intrepid a journey as the menu, and the bar snacks provide sumptuous wee samples of what goes on in the kitchen. Stay the night in one of the two guest rooms, and you'll have a chance the next morning to rent a bicycle for a countryside sojourn. In keeping with the major theme, even the bikes are made from recycled coffee pods.

Address 10 Crimp Hill, Old Windsor SL4 2QY, +44 (0)1753 851470, www.lochandtyne.com | Getting there Bus 8 from York House to Toby Carvery, then a 15-minute walk; by road take the A308 South, right onto St Peter's Road, then right onto Crimp Hill | Hours Wed 5pm–midnight, Thu–Sun noon–midnight (but check website for times of food service) | Tip Make it a pub crawl by popping your head into The Union Inn Hotel next door, with its delightful timber-framed bar and roaring fireplace.

59 Market Cross
The local news broadcast

Head back to John Norden's 1607 maps of Windsor and you'll notice the street plan has barely changed. One notable exception, however, is the loss of the Market Cross. Built by John Sadler in 1380 and illustrated by Norden as a Tudor-style building on timber stilts, it once stood at the junction of Peascod Street and Castle Hill. For 300 years, Market Cross marked the epicentre of urban life in Windsor, home to everything from trade to local politics, but when the Guildhall came along in 1689 it was deemed redundant and torn down. The lone memory of its name can be seen above the Crooked House (see ch. 22), which is officially titled 'Market Cross House'.

However, there is a Market Cross tradition that continues to this day. While ambling around Windsor on certain days – especially in the wake of, or build-up to some momentous event – you may hear the words 'Oyez! Oyez!' ringing out. This signifies that Chris Brown, Windsor's official town crier, is about to make a declaration.

In an age before newspapers, the town crier fulfilled the essential role of keeping the town informed about local goings-on. Records of Windsor's town criers go back as far as 1666, but it's likely the role was established long before then. Many of these criers throughout history would have made their declarations from Market Cross, and with great respect to the legacy, Chris often makes his own announcements from the same site.

Dressed in traditional robes and tricorn hat, wielding a re-creation of the Windsor Bell used by local criers since time immemorial, Chris relies solely on his booming voice to carry his messages (he claims a good belt of Port every now and then helps keep his throat lubricated). If you close your eyes, you can almost imagine you're back in medieval Windsor, standing in the shadow of Market Cross, perhaps learning that Henry VIII had taken yet another wife.

Address Castle Hill, Windsor SL4 1PD, www.windsortowncrier.com | Getting there Train to either Windsor & Eton Central or Windsor & Eton Riverside, then a five-minute walk; served by most bus routes | Hours See the website for a timetable of Chris' upcoming declarations | Tip The original site of Market Cross is now home to Sir Joseph Edgar Boehm's statue of Queen Victoria. Unveiled in 1887, it has since become a worthy successor as the town's most iconic centrepiece.

60 Monkey Island

Monkey in the middle of the Thames

To answer your first question: no, to the best of my knowledge, no real monkeys can be found on this island. But before you start Googling 'false advertising', know that the name 'Monkey' actually derives from 'Monks' Eyot'. The meaning behind this name is just as mysterious, for no monasteries existed in the area, but it may have had something to do with nearby Burnham Abbey, as the name was briefly recorded as 'Bournhames Eyte' in the 14th century.

In any case, this diddy river island was relatively insignificant (much less inhabitable) until after the Great Fire of London. As part of Sir Christopher Wren's plan to rebuild the city out of stone, the Thames at this time became an essential route for the transport of materials to the city, and for the removal of rubble in the other direction. On the return leg, boats would dump their waste on this low-lying ait, slowly transforming it from a boggy mudflat into a substantial islet.

This made Monkey Island suddenly very attractive to Charles Spencer, 3rd Duke of Marlborough, who bought it in 1723 to transform into his own private fishing paradise. To that end, he employed architect Robert Morris to design two majestic manors: the Pavilion and the Temple. In keeping with the major theme, much monkey business ensued: the Pavilion was made from wooden blocks made to imitate stone, while the Temple, designed as a sort of giant aquarium, houses a farcical fresco by Andien de Clermont depicting monkeys taking part in high society activities such as punting and shooting.

Today, the island is owned by Malaysian hotel firm YTL, whose chairman Tan Sri Yeoh Lay spared its Grade I-listed edifices from the indignity of dilapidation. Sadly, he did not live to see the opening of his hotel, but the project was finished by his sons who added a dignified statue of their father to welcome visitors crossing the footbridge.

Address Monkey Island Estate, Bray SL6 2EE, +44 (0)1628 623400, www.monkeyislandestate.co.uk | Getting there By car, from Bray High Street, follow Old Mill Lane to Monkey Island Lane. Cross the M4 motorway bridge, then follow signs to Monkey Island Estate, where you will find a car park on the mainland near the footbridge. | Hours Although the island is not open to the general public, you can get a view of it from the water. Alternatively, treat yourself to a luxury weekend. | Tip On the Bray side of the footbridge is a notable white timber-framed house called Long White Cloud. This was the childhood home of Sir Stirling Moss, winner of 16 Formula One Grand Prix.

61 Montem Mound
Earth of the salt

Have you always dreamed of being inducted into Eton College? Well, now you can be. Grab a salt shaker, your favourite Latin poem, and head to the summit of this mysterious wee hillock to recreate one of Eton's barmiest traditions.

Here's the backstory: on the morning of Whit Tuesday, the road from Eton College to Montem Mound would be lined with onlookers. *'Floreat Etona!'* ('May Eton Flourish!') they'd cry, as the boys marched past, dressed in military regalia or fancy dress, with the monarch of the day leading the troop under the banner of the Royal Standard.

When they got to the hill, the seniors would belt out a chorus of Latin anthems, then take handfuls of salt and rub them vigorously into the faces of their juniors, in a sort of quasi-religious hazing practice. The excess salt would then be handed out to onlookers in return for donations – the monarch was expected to give a particularly generous gift, while anyone who didn't cough up would be chased down and have their mouth filled with the stuff.

No one knows how or when this popular procession (known as *'Ad Montem'*) started, although legend has it this was once part of the school's subversive election of a 'boy-bishop'. Indeed, the original ceremony had the students perform a scandalous sermon, one that so offended Queen Charlotte she begged it to stop. Later, the funds raised from *Ad Montem* went to the College's top academic to pay for his tuition at Cambridge. But the tradition ended abruptly in 1847, probably due to bad behaviour, and has not returned since.

Over the centuries, the College remained blissfully ignorant of the significance of their revered knoll. That was until 2016, when a team from the University of Reading discovered Montem Mound to be an early Saxon burial mound of unusually large size, suggesting it was connected to a powerful local king – and probably chock-full of treasure.

Address Montem Lane, Slough SL1 2QG | Getting there Train to Slough (Elizabeth Line), then a 15-minute walk; bus 4, 5, 6, 13, 103 or X74 to Windmill Road, or 83 to Salt Hill Three Tuns; free parking at Slough Ice Arena | Tip Head back along Bath Road to Slough High Street to find Mori, which is easily the best restaurant in Slough, and possibly some of the best Japanese cuisine you'll find in the whole of England.

62 moogBrew

Puts the 'tap' in Taplow

Sometime after the smoking ban came into effect, it became dread-fully trendy for pubs to have 'secret beer gardens'. These invariably take the form of a converted hollow between the pub's back wall and some adjacent building, with just enough room for a picnic bench. Gardens they ain't, and given the fact they are usually advertised on the pub's A-frames, one must also question whether they are truly secret. A real secret beer garden ought to be just that: a secret, the kind a man in a trench coat passes you in a manila envelope; and a garden, the kind with grass and flowers and bumblebees humming in the summer. Better still if the beer element is taken seriously too. To discover what a real secret beer garden looks like, make the short pilgrimage to moogBrew.

Husband and wife Id and Margi were pioneers of the British craft beer movement. After travelling the USA and the Low Countries for inspiration, they returned to England to start their own label in moogBrew. With cult comic artist Dave Anderson providing the branding, Id and Margi became big names in the beer-making scene. But, unlike many of their peers, the couple wanted to keep moogBrew a purely home-brewed affair. So, instead of expanding their enter-prise and shipping worldwide, they decided to sell the product out of their own back garden.

With the blessing of their neighbours, Id and Margi have been pouring moogBrew from their summer house in Taplow since 2017. The beer itself is brewed just 20 yards away in their garage, and the taps change every season so that there is always some new concoction on offer. Beer lovers will find themselves in paradise, with oodles of whacky flavours to choose from, whether the aniseedy *In Bruges* or the grapefruit punch of *Five-Citra*. Come, relax, sample everything on the menu, and make Id and Margi's garden your own – just, please, keep it a secret.

Address Meads End, Ye Meads, Taplow SL6 06H, +44 (0)7941 241954, www.moogbrew.co.uk | Getting there Train from Slough to Taplow (Elizabeth Line), then a 15-minute walk; bus 8 from Arthur Lane to Slough High Street, then bus 4 from Queensmere Car Park towards Maidenhead, alight at Marsh Lane, then a 10-minute walkTrain from Slough to Taplow (Elizabeth Line), then a 15-minute walk; bus 8 from Arthur Lane to Slough High Street, then bus 4 from Queensmere Car Park towards Maidenhead, alight at Marsh Lane, then a 10-minute walk | Hours These vary, so check the website or follow @moogBrew on Instagram and X for upcoming dates | Tip If you've arrived a bit early, stop by Taplow Lake to discover Lake House Café. Sit on the terrace and watch the water skiers and the kayakers – heck, why not get involved yourself? (Visit www.taplowlakeside.co.uk).

63 Museum of Antiquities

A modern home for ancient treasures

One of the advantages of being Eton College is that your school is forever connected to a network of some of the most influential scholars on the planet. Eton has produced many an intellectual over the years; so, too, has it produced many adventurers (shout-out to Bear Grylls). Smush the two together, and what do you get? Journeymen archaeologists in the style of Indiana Jones. Lord Roberts of Kandahar, Major William J. Myers and George Herbert, fifth Earl of Carnarvon are some of many well-travelled alumni who have contributed gifts of ancient magnificence to their Alma Mater over the years. Theirs and many other pieces can be seen in the school's own Museum of Antiquities.

The Jafar Gallery, which houses the museum, is a small but perfectly formed space. John Simpson's Neo-classical design pours emphasis on the neo, for the building was created as recently as 2016. What a relief to find a 21st-century building that doesn't rely on fake brick cladding and angular geometry. Instead, we get intricate brickwork, a bronze roof and semi-circular, floor-to-ceiling windows that beam light into the museum within.

This is the museum's seventh venue, which might explain why it hasn't had the time to focus on growing its collection. Still, the pieces on display in these 12 cabinets are all killer, no filler. They are the kinds of materials you would expect to see in a big city museum, only in a more boutique quantity. Visitors are spared verbose interpretations lurking in the corners of the cabinets – artefacts are displayed mute, allowing individuals to arrive at their own conclusions, although elucidation can be found in one of the free pocket guide books.

The centrepiece is an Egyptian statue base bearing the cartouche of Ramesses II, which forms a neat link to the poem *Ozymandias* by Old Etonian Percy Bysshe Shelley – a vast and trunkless leg of stone indeed.

Address The Jafar Gallery, South Meadow Lane, Eton SL4 6EW, The Jafar Gallery, South Meadow Lane, Eton SL4 6EW, +44 (0)1753 370590, collections.etoncollege.com/ museums/museum-of-antiquities | Getting there Train to either Windsor & Eton Riverside or Windsor & Eton Central, then a 15-minute walk; bus 15, 63 or 68 to Keats Lane; by car, nearby pay and display parking at Meadow Lane Car Park (SL4 6BN) | Hours Sun 2.30–5pm | Tip The walk back into town through South Meadow offers excellent views of Windsor Castle. Stop by the Church of St John the Evangelist on your way for a moment's rest in the garden.

64__Museum of Eton Life

Not your average day at school

It's astounding to think that life at one particular school could be so radically different as to warrant its own museum. But then there is no comparison to life at Eton College. Whether it's the hallways they traipse or the sports they play, the clothes they wear or the lessons they take, everything a boy will experience in his years at Eton is remarkable, not to mention somewhat mysterious. How fitting, then, that the experience of getting to this museum is cryptic in itself – the setting, like the Slytherin common room, is in the college's undercroft, which can only be reached on non-school days via a secret side entrance.

The major theme of the museum is, of course, life. In this respect, it over-achieves. The strict, almost militaristic living standards of Etonians are laid bare, with no punches pulled. From a display illustrating the students' utilitarian bedrooms, to a passage on the school's regretful history of corporal punishment, the museum is keenly aware of the elements that make Eton College so fascinating to the outside observer.

Many of these elements – such as the tribal adherence to colour-coding every society, or the speeches given in Latin at the 4 June celebrations – may seem somewhat barmy. The museum gleefully leans into this weirdness, arguing that while they appear anachronistic in modern society, a dogmatic adherence to tradition is one of the cornerstones of an Eton education.

Of course, the museum has another purpose, which is to advertise the school's many achievements. Sport is one aspect it is keen to highlight. Coming away, you will be aware that the college has produced 15 Olympic gold medal winners, has won two FA Cups, and is credited with the invention of modern football. The copywriter in me wishes they had sealed the deal with a call to action: 'Sign your child up today! Prices start at £45,000 per year.'

Address Brewhouse Yard, Baldwin's Shore, Eton, Windsor SL4 6DB, +44 (0)1753 370590, collections.etoncollege.com/museums/museum-of-eton-life | **Getting there** Look for the large wooden door on Baldwin's Shore, then follow signs through the courtyard. Train to Windsor & Eton Riverside, then a 10-minute walk, or to Windsor & Eton Central and a 15-minute walk; bus 15, 63 or 68 to Eton College. | **Hours** Sun 2.30–5pm | **Tip** Be sure to swing by the Verey Gallery in the main courtyard round the corner. This is also a good chance to get up close and personal to Lupton's Tower and the statue of King Henry VI, which are usually off-limits to the public.

65 Natural History Museum

You can't have skeleton without Eton

A stained-glass portrait of Charles Darwin, hand-painted by former curator Dr David Smith, looks down upon the scene. Nearby, just beyond the Giant Sea Turtle, is Smith's favourite exhibit, a taxidermied Kākāpō – a flightless parrot sourced from as far afield as New Zealand.

The displays continue in this manner, crammed so full of exotic species that vulnerable birds and tiny rodents are forced to share a cabinet with sly foxes. It may seem a million miles from the wide Gothic hallways of its South Kensington namesake, yet Eton's Natural History Museum punches well above its featherweight constitution. Nor is the setting any less splendid, occupying an extension of the Lower Chapel, complete with a domed turret and obligatory spiral staircase.

Like any good natural history museum, it's a real horrorshow. If you've never seen the skeleton of an ostrich, let your imagination not decide for you – there's no way you could guess the right number of vertebrae in that freakishly long neck. And oh god, the moths, *the moths!*

There is local intrigue among these cases, the prime example being the tusk of a hairy mammoth dredged from the Thames in Boveney. So too is there human interest: artefacts brought back from the Penan tribe in Borneo's Sarawak region by Old Etonian Robin Hanbury-Tenison include a never-ending penis sheath and a Parang sword alleged to have chopped off 100 heads. Nearby is the slightly more wholesome story of Mary Anning, 'the greatest fossil hunter ever known', who, with her loyal pooch Tray, pulled up hundreds of rare relics from the sands around her hometown of Lyme Regis.

Downstairs, a faithful reconstruction of Eton boy Sir Joseph Banks' cabin on the HMB *Endeavour* is intended to appeal to younger visitors. It fails in its ambition though, as children instead make a beeline for the grosser, ghastlier sides of the museum; Darwin smirks knowingly.

Address South Meadow Lane, Eton SL4 6EW, collections.etoncollege.com/museums/ natural-history-museum | **Getting there** Train to either Windsor & Eton Riverside or Windsor & Eton Central, then a 15-minute walk; bus 15, 63 or 68 to Keats Lane; by car, nearby pay and display parking at Meadow Lane Car Park (SL4 6BN) | **Hours** Sun 2.30–5pm | **Tip** I love the Eton Wick Road Chapel, not too far from this gallery. Designed by James Deason in the Gothic style, its flint walls with Bath stone dressings make it simple, yet charming.

66 New Lodge

Kings just wanna have fun

When James VI of Scotland also became James I of England, his vulgar reputation travelled south with him. Despite his many achievements, James' popular image was of a slurring drunk and an impulsive decision maker with a bad habit of appointing his favourite handsome men to senior positions.

Which brings us to New Lodge. While the present Gothic Revival building (which sadly can only be seen from a distance, since the estate is private) was erected in 1857 by the architect Thomas Talbot Bury, the original site housed a lodge believed to date to the early 1500s. During James' reign, it stood at the centre of 'New Lodge Walk', a hunting park that has entered popular folklore as the setting of a Broadside Ballad by an unknown author, titled 'King James and the Tinker'.

The story goes thus: King James is out hunting one day, but grows bored and gives his noblemen the slip. He winds up at a pub, where he meets a tinker (a travelling tinsmith) who doesn't recognise the king. The two bond over several jugs of 'nappy brown ale' until the tinker confides that he has always dreamt of seeing the king in the flesh. This gives James an idea – he tells the tinker to ride with him, and the first man he sees wearing a hood will be the king. The two depart to New Lodge, where James' noblemen are waiting – but they are all bareheaded. Suddenly, the tinker realises that his new drinking partner is wearing a hood. He drops to his knees, but King James orders him to arise, knighting him on the spot and proffering him a salary of 500 crowns.

At first glance, it seems an uplifting tale and a positive reflection on James' flamboyantly generous persona. But look closer, and you'll see that it paints a satirical portrait of the king's many vices. Not only does he sneak off to go out on the pish, he ends up coming home with a stray peasant and an annual bill of 500 crowns!

Address Drift Road, Winkfield SL4 4RR, www.newlodgewindsor.co.uk | **Getting there** Can be viewed from Drift Road | **Hours** Viewable from the outside only | **Tip** The pub where King James was alleged to have met the tinker was The Royal Black Bridge, which is sadly long gone. But you can re-enact their famous meeting at the nearby Fifield Inn.

67___Norden Farm

Farmcore theatre

Whether by cows or concerts, Norden Farm has played an essential role in the lives of Maidenheaders since times of olde. No one is quite sure how long this former dairy farm has been here. It appears on all the oldest maps – in fact I wouldn't be surprised if it was somewhere on *Mappa Mundi*. What we can be sure of is that, after the milk ran dry, the farm has been producing an equally important commodity: entertainment.

Getting to opening day was a helluva struggle. As far back as 1978, Maidenhead Arts – an umbrella organisation representing a collective of local societies – had been looking for a permanent home. Fourteen years would pass before an opportunity presented itself when, in 1992, the local council offered up the 18th-century buildings at Norden Farm on the proviso that the proprietors would establish a theatre. Right up our street, thought the collective, and so the gears started turning. Arts Council funding came in 1994, and then finally – *finally* – the new Norden Farm opened on 17 September, 2000.

Truly, the centre has made fine use of its historic buildings. The old barn offers a shabby-chic wedding venue, while the grand Georgian farmhouse stars as the centre's head offices. As for the rest of the complex, well… in the absence of a suitable descriptor, I hereby coin the phrase 'rusto-modernist' to describe the aesthetic. See the café, for instance: a swooping concrete-and-glass façade on one side, rugged brick on the other, and an ultra-high timber ceiling in between.

At the centre of the venue is the sunken theatre, with a retractable stage and 220 seats watching a conveyor belt of bums pass by, coming for a comedy show one night, a cinema screening the next, maybe even a folk gig. Not that these are the only reasons to visit: elsewhere, you'll find art classes, mindfulness sessions and, on the first Saturday of the month, an artisan market.

Address Altwood Road, Maidenhead SL6 4PF, +44 (0)1628 788997,
https://norden.farm | **Getting there** Train to Maidenhead (Elizabeth Line), then a
25-minute walk; bus 3, 127, 234, 235, 238, 239 or F 10 to Bath Road Cricket Ground, then
a 10-minute walk via Wootton Way to Altwood Road; free parking on site | Hours Varies –
plan your trip by visiting https://norden.farm/opening-times | Tip Head back to the town
centre to get your second dose of local culture at the delightful Maidenhead Heritage
Centre (www.maidenheadheritage.org.uk).

68 Oakley Court

Transylvania-on-Thames

Nary a day goes by when you won't see an Instagrammable wedding happening on the lawn of Oakley Court, such is its grandeur. But it's not just beauty this building has in heaps – it's intrigue, too.

That intrigue starts at the beginning, of which very little is known. The early history? Lost. The architect? Unknown. It's as if this castle appeared from the fog, or rose up from the underworld. Legend has it one of the early proprietors, Sir Richard Hall Say, had it built in 1859 in the style of a grand château for his homesick French wife. The French connection may have some legs: it later found its way into the hands of *La Résistance*, even playing host to Charles de Gaulle himself.

After the war, the building was abandoned. The dilapidation only added to its appeal though, and it soon caught the eye of production house Hammer Films. Oakley Court became their muse, their flame, catalysing their transition into the horror genre, which they would soon revolutionise. Peter Cushing spent a lot of time spilling blood and guts at Oakley Court, first as Dr Frankenstein in *The Curse of Frankenstein,* then as John Banning in *The Mummy* and later as Van Helsing sorting out *The Brides of Dracula* – poor Christopher Lee was usually on the receiving end.

Such was the success of Hammer they moved to their own pur-pose-built studio next door, but their leftover props were put to good use by Tim Curry, whose Dr Frank-N-Furter did the Time Warp Again here in *The Rocky Horror Picture Show,* and Peter Cook, who arrived as Sherlock Holmes to figure out the mystery of *The Hound of the Baskervilles.*

Today, the building houses a hotel with interiors lovingly revamped (geddit?) by Alex Eagle and a Japanese *omakase* restaurant headed up by Akira Shimizu. You can even hire their boats for pleasure cruises down the Thames – just be sure to keep an eye out for vampires, mummies and werewolves.

Address Windsor Road, Water Oakley, Windsor SL4 5UR, +44 (0)1753 609988, www.oakleycourt.co.uk | Getting there Public transport is lacking in this area, so the best way to get here is by car – look for signs along the A308. | Tip If you're staying at the hotel during the summer, pay a visit to Bray Lake up the road, where you'll find plenty of watersports to enjoy (www.braylake.com).

69___ The Old Court

Vintage cinema

A waft of piano tones serenades you through the front door. Turn right and you're at the bar, serving up Windsor & Eton Brewery's finest. Turn left and make your way past the pop-up gallery selling local artists' paintings into the airy cinema hall to watch the latest arthouse or Bollywood film. Upstairs is a conference room painted in graffiti, downstairs a dance studio-cum-events hall, technicolour lights giving an ironic school disco feel to what was once a World War II nuclear washdown station.

This is The Old Court, Windsor's own arts and cultural space, and one of the town's proudest achievements. Its story goes back to 1973, when a group of local campaigners connected to the Windsor Fringe took charge of an unloved civic building that once housed a magistrate's court, a police station and a fire station.

The Grade II-listed edifice, dating to 1905, is an eye-catching mish-mash of both the Edwardian and Queen Anne Revival styles, a jigsaw of red brick and white stone with a particularly gorgeous incarnation of the Royal Crest perched above its stained-glass windows. The interior, meanwhile, is all modernised, which is necessary to cater to the diverse range of activities The Old Court has to offer. Upon every visit, you will be greeted with something different going on, whether it's a jazz and swing dance session, live music, drama classes or even a wedding.

The punk undercurrent that helped to establish this space is subtle, and perhaps best embodied in the bar, which is typically packed out with students and hipsters who spill out of the doors meant for fire engines onto the sun-drenched terrace during the summer. For the ultimate experience, come for a throw-back night at the cinema. Grab yourself a themed cocktail, take your pew in the auditorium, and listen closely to hear the heartbeat of Windsor's electric arts and cultural scene.

Address St Leonard's Road, Windsor SL4 3BL, +44 (0)1753 911333, www.oldcourt.org |
Getting there Train to Windsor & Eton Riverside, then a 15-minute walk, or Windsor
Central and a 10-minute walk; bus 1, W 1, 2, 8, 9, 10, 16, 600, 702 or 703 | Hours Mon–Wed
11am–10pm, Thu & Fri 11am–11pm, Sat 10am–11pm, Sun 10am–10.30pm | Tip The
Old Court takes up half of the original building – the other half is now serviced offices. Peek
round the corner of St Mark's Place to see what was once the Chief Constable's private house.

70 Pavement Clock
What's the time, Mr Pavement?

Most people pass along Thames Street in a daze, captivated by the mighty Curfew Tower. At 100 feet high, and with a history dating back to the Siege of Windsor in 1216, it surely steals the status of most awe-inspiring bastion at Windsor Castle. And if those pedestrians wanted to know the time? Well then, they need only look to the bell cage above the parapets, where the Curfew Clock has kept Windsor running like clockwork since 1478.

But die-hard clock-watchers would do better to look beneath their feet, for there they would find the Pavement Clock. Installed in 1950 by Royal Clockmaker (and later Mayor of Windsor) Sir Cyril Dyson, this sunken chronometer gave Windsor the coveted status of 'only town in the UK with a clock in the pavement', which is… cool, I guess? Why precisely Mr Dyson decided to stick an illuminated clock in the pavement is a mystery. Perhaps he was following the fashion set by William Barthman, who had tried a similar marketing stunt outside his Manhattan jewellery store in 1898.

Two people for whom the clock has immense significance are David and Theresa Chapman, who arranged to meet here for their first date in 1985 – a night that would ultimately lead to a long and happy marriage. After discovering that it had been quietly removed some years later, Theresa wrote a tear-jerking letter to the local newspaper that sparked a campaign to restore this iconic clock.

A replacement, by Good Directions Ltd of Hampshire, arrived in 2011. Mayor Catherine Bursnall and Dyson's granddaughter Caroline Fox unveiled the second edition, but not before popping a time capsule underneath. Like the previous model, the new clock has already taken a beating, and is prone to condensation build-up during the wetter seasons. Still, the Footway Clock remains an enduring symbol of Windsor – still the only town in Britain with a clock in the pavement.

Address Outside Thai Terrace, 9 Thames Street, Windsor SL4 1PL | Getting there Train to either Windsor & Eton Central or Windsor & Eton Riverside, then a five-minute walk from both; served by most bus routes | Tip Look for the hidden alleyway to Curfew Yard, where you can enjoy a quiet coffee and a cake at Cup of Rosie (www.cup-of-rosie.com), in a beautiful building dating from 1628.

71 Queen Mary's Dolls' House
Elegance writ small

Heralded as the greatest British architect of all time, Sir Edwin Lutyens' globetrotting career spread the Arts and Crafts vernacular across the British Isles, Europe and even India. Lutyens was a master of materials, combining brick, stone and glass with landscape design to produce everything from country manors to war memorials. Among his greatest works, Lutyens lists the Cenotaph in London, the Thiepval Memorial in France and India Gate, New Delhi.

Yet the piece he is best remembered for is not any of his monolithic monuments or scenic manor houses. Rather, it is this kitsch mansion-in-miniature, commissioned by the cousin of King George V, Princess Marie Louise, for his wife Queen Mary. Every detail is crafted with painstaking precision, such that the house acts not just as a charming bit of whimsy, but as an accurate reconstruction of royal life in early modern England. Dozens of skilled artisans were employed to produce its 1,500 pocket-sized fittings at 1:12 scale. Among them were some significant names: Peter Waals designed the furnishings; Sir William Orpen painted the royal portraits; the gardens were landscaped by Gertrude Jekyll; and the library is stocked with books containing specially written stories by Sir Arthur Conan Doyle, A. A. Milne and Rudyard Kipling.

The whole piece took three years to make and was unveiled at the British Empire Exhibition of 1924 before moving to Windsor Castle. It may seem sorrowful to see this majestic dolls' house locked away behind glass. The uncomfortable perfection begs for a child's imaginative fingers to animate the scene. But it is important to remember the piece was a gift to the nation, a representation of British inventiveness and togetherness in the wake of World War I. Perhaps one day it will be given to a child who can bring it to life – to make it the beloved toy it yearns to be.

Address Windsor Castle, Windsor SL4 1NJ, www.rct.uk/visit/windsor-castle | **Getting there** Follow the visitor's trail around Windsor Castle | **Hours** 1 Mar–31 Oct 10am–5.15pm (last admission 4pm); 1 Nov–28 Feb 10am–4.15pm (last admission 3pm) | **Tip** If you're in the mood for more miniatures, be sure to make the Moat Room part of your trail. There, you will find a scale bronze model of Windsor Castle as it would have appeared in 1377.

72 __ The Royal Stag
The pub with its own tombstone

Known first as Churchlands, then The Bridge House, then The Five Bells and finally The Royal Stag, this building has been the beating heart of Datchet since 1494. Before becoming a pub, it played an even more important role: maintaining the bridge over Piller's Pond, a swampy lake now covered by Datchet Memorial Green.

The building's best-known owner was Robert Barker, Royal Printer to King James I, who made one of history's greatest blunders: he forgot to put the 'not' in 'thou shalt not commit adultery' in his first run of the King James Bible. Never mind that, for here in Datchet he is remembered in more heroic terms as the man behind the Barker Bridge House Trust. This trust, which still exists today, not only paid for the upkeep of the aforementioned bridge, it also built the turnpike road to Colnbrook, provided new buildings for the High Street, and remodelled the church and graveyard.

Speaking of which, it's hard to miss that the pub overlooks a graveyard. This has, naturally, spawned a number of ghost stories over the years. The first concerns the gravestone of William Herbert, which has somehow made its way indoors and can now be found propped up against the back wall. Rumour has it this is one of many such tombstones taken from the graveyard, the rest of which make up the floor of the cellar. This seems… actually kinda likely. If the churchyard was overflowing with stones like William's at the same time the pub was being remodelled, why not take advantage of the free materials, right?

The other big mystery concerns the window facing the graveyard where, despite numerous attempts to clean it, a ghostly child's handprint is said to appear. Like any good ghost story, the origin of the myth changes according to the speaker, but is usually some variant of a tale in which a boy freezes to death in the churchyard while waiting for his father to finish getting drunk. Seems like a cautionary tale: it's always safer to be inside the pub on a cold night.

Address The Green, Datchet SL3 9JH, +44 (0)1753 584231, www.royalstagdatchet.com |
Getting there Train to Datchet | **Hours** Daily 11am–midnight | **Tip** Datchet is unique
in having three war memorials, all in different styles. See if you can find them all: one is a
crucifix; the women's memorial is a Celtic cross; and the last and most prominent is an obelisk.

73 — The Running Man
Always look on the bright side of life

Close your eyes and picture Jesus on the cross. What do you see? The grievous look of pain? The crown of thorns piercing his skull? The blood dashed across his frail body? Well, according to this statue of Christ atop the tower of All Saints' Church in Dedworth, you'd be wrong, wrong and wrong. Here we see Jesus bounding away from his crucifixion, limbs akimbo, wearing not a crown of thorns but a victory garland, a euphoric smile across his face. Overlooking the obvious meme potential, the piece has a heartwarming history: it was designed in 2010 by local artist Gill Ledsham with the help of over 200 students from Windsor Boys' School. Positive, upbeat and loving were some of the words that informed the brief, and the finished product hits those marks – the *Church Times* described Jesus as looking 'like a goal-scoring footballer'.

The statue encapsulates the soul of All Saints, a place where worship is made colourful by an abundance of art. A whirl around the building reveals a technicolour dreamscape. The Link Room is painted with murals by local artist Carolyn Carter depicting scenes from Jesus' life, while floor-to-ceiling murals in the hall, also by Carter, tell the stories of the Crucifixion and Resurrection (this time, Jesus doesn't look so chipper). *The Running Man* even has a cousin – another sculpture by Ledsham in The Porch depicts the Virgin Mary embracing her sister-in-law Elizabeth.

Meanwhile, in the foyer, a matchstick model by church member Terry Skinner shows what the building once looked like – the previous Victorian church fell to pieces and had to be replaced by this modernist iteration in 1972. Mercifully, many of the original windows (including three designed by the firm of William Morris) survive, and have been expertly incorporated into the new building. Like *The Running Man* himself, the whole church is a symbol of happy rebirth.

Address Dedworth Road, Windsor SL4 4JW, www.allsaintschurchdedworth.com | Getting there Bus 2 or W1 to All Saints Church, or 16 to The Maypole; free parking on-site | Hours Mon – Fri 9am – 5pm, Sunday Gathering 9.15 and 11am | Tip Another Windsor church that sadly passed away was the Church of the Saviour on Bier Lane (now River Street). The lych gate is the only part of the church that survives, and can be found at the entrance of the nearby Clewer Memorial Park.

74_ Savill Garden

The definitive English country garden

There is something embedded deep in the British DNA that draws us all, sooner or later, to gardening. The archetype of this national spirit was Sir Eric Savill who, from 1932 to 1951, reached the apex of landscape design with this, the jewel in the Great Park's already heavily-encrusted crown.

Before Sir Eric arrived, the earth beneath this land was sandy, waterlogged and tree-riddled. It took a visionary of extraordinary calibre to ascertain that the moist earth and the natural canopies offered by the dense forest would make the perfect environment for a bountiful garden chock full of exotic plants.

The genesis of Sir Eric's vision came to him as a child, when he would spend countless hours walking the Great Park – and it was at this time he became acutely aware of the lack of flowers across the landscape. After a stint on the frontlines of World War I, Sir Eric went into the family business of land surveying, but a fated job application brought him instead to the Great Park, where he immediately parlayed with King George V to create his dream garden. George agreed speculatively, but could not spare an ounce of budget, and so Sir Eric made do by trading the rabbits he had snared with local horticulturalists. When George and Queen Mary saw the first draft of what was then called The Bog Garden, they were suitably impressed, and even asked Sir Eric to expand the garden all the way up to the 34 acres it is today. When the garden was complete, George deemed it worthy of bearing Sir Eric's name, and thus the Savill Garden was inaugurated.

Sir Eric's aim was simply to plant as many flowers as possible, which he certainly achieved. There are too many species to name individually, but it is not any one individual breed that stands out, rather the full spectacle: a chromatic explosion in year-round bloom, a feast for the eyes as well as the nose.

Address Wick Lane, Englefield Green TW20 0UJ, +44 (0)1753 860222, www.windsorgreatpark.co.uk/the-savill-garden | Getting there By car, from the A30, follow Wick Road onto Wick Lane – parking available on-site | Hours Daily 9am–6pm | Tip Another visionary who took advantage of the Great Park's waterlogged earth was Henry Flitcroft, who created the serene ornamental lake known as the Cow Pond. Follow the path north from the Savill Garden Visitor Centre to find it lurking in the hedgerows.

75 Southlea Farm

Old Old Windsor?

Sometimes a juxtaposition can seem so pointed it approaches irony. That is certainly the case at this meander of the Thames. On the west bank lies the splendour of Home Park, centuries of landscaping shaping an area now solely for the pleasure of the Royal Family, replete with a golf course and an eventing arena. Then, on the east side is, err, just a farm.

But, aha, had you fooled. For Southlea Farm is not just any farm. It is, in fact, an area of unprecedented local historical importance, the site of one of the country's best-preserved prehistoric landscapes and a treasure trove of archaeological bits 'n' bobs. This was revealed between 1996 and 2008 by the Datchet Village Society, an amateur local history group. Led by Janet Kennish, who became interested in the site after stumbling upon aerial photographs revealing some mysterious patterns beneath the crops, the team embarked on a field-work investigation that ended up uncovering find after find, each one building a more complete picture of what was ultimately discovered to be a substantial ancient settlement. In fact, the continuity of finds, dating through the Mesolithic to the Romano-British periods, suggests that this patch of land was inhabited throughout prehistory until at least the beginning of the Saxon era.

To the ancient visitor, the site would have been marked by great barrows jutting out of the floodplains forming a path towards an enclosed village of roundhouses. This was not only the centre of local power, but perhaps also acted as a livestock market, and was home to a number of skilled artisans whose thousands of shards of pottery and metalworks have survived long enough to make their way into a permanent display at the Datchet Library.

There is indeed a great irony here, that for all the pomp put on by its neighbours, it is Southlea Farm that lays the best claim to being the most historic land in Windsor.

Address Southlea Farm, Datchet SL3 9DA | **Getting there** The Thames Path crosses Albert Bridge and runs through the south of the farm; train to Datchet, then a 15-minute walk; bus 5, 305, 703 or P 1 to Datchet, then a 15-minute walk | **Hours** Accessible 24 hours | **Tip** Crossing the Thames just south of the farm is Albert Bridge. Part-designed by Prince Albert and built in 1851, it was intended to redirect traffic away from Home Park, which had been sealed off from the public by the earlier Windsor Castle Act of 1848.

76 Splash Mill

The wacky windmill of Wraysbury

What would you do if the council denied you planning permission to build a house? If you were Glyn Larcombe, you would find the loopiest of loopholes and build a windmill instead. Because here's the thing: so long as your structure is not, strictly speaking, 'permanent' – say for instance you built it out of wood in a caravan plot – the paper-pushers can't stop you. Glyn one, council nil.

Thanks to that moment of genius (or spite?), this tower now stands proud over Wraysbury. At first, it looks antique, but it was actually built in 1996. Its dated appearance is thanks to the fact it is made of reclaimed dockland wood: weathered and warped from centuries spent floating in the water, it gives the edifice an authentic rickety impression. It even uses an old truck axle as the rotor for the turbine. So, it's a recycled windmill. How fashionable.

Today, the building is maintained by engineer-slash-artist Wayne Herbert, who is constantly updating it with new, quirky features. Pop your head into The Perseverance pub next door and you might bump into him – he's always keen to show people around his beloved home. If you thought the building looked impressive from the outside, wait 'til you get in the front door.

Like something out of a Hayao Miyazaki film, light pours in from 360-degree windows, illuminating hidden corners hiding all manner of trinkets. The wood creaks ominously when a gust of wind blows, but rest assured the ghostly girl you hear singing lullabies is a cheeky feature Wayne installed himself. Its five floors of vaulted ceilings and wood floors almost lure you into thinking you're in a Tudor home, but then you remember you're in a windmill, an honest to God windmill.

How poetic, that in sticking a middle finger up to bureaucracy, Larcombe ended up creating Wraysbury's most iconic centrepiece. Let us all aspire to be so imaginative in our dissent.

Address The Green, Wraysbury TW19 5NA | Getting there Train to Wraysbury; bus 305 to Wraysbury High Street | Hours Not open to the public, but can be seen from The Green in Wraysbury | Tip Wayne's favourite pub, The Perseverance (aka 'The Percy'), is a 17th-century beaut that serves up a range of rare ales and a delicious menu of home cooked meals, including a show-stopping Sunday lunch.

77 — St Andrew's, Clewer

The church history couldn't keep up with

It's a big flex to be able to call yourself the oldest building in Windsor. Yet, despite the fact no one can be sure how old this church is exactly, you wouldn't doubt it to step inside. Barely an inch of wall remains that doesn't house a plaque telling the story of some interesting person who has worshipped here (William the Conqueror himself is believed to have been a regular). Even on a gloomy day, the vibrant colours and copious amounts of gold make the church so illuminated as to render it dazzling, and barely a drop of rain will touch you as you walk around the grounds, so thick are the ancient yew trees standing over the gravestones.

Of the many interesting things to note, let us start outside, where the outer walls are built from chalk taken from the cliff upon which Windsor Castle was later built. That same chalk gave its name to Clewer, which in Old English means 'cliff dwellers'. The chapel, alleged to have been built on top of the central barrow in a formation extending from Beaconsfield to Chobham, was a gift from Sir Bernard Brocas and houses the Saxon font plus a stained-glass window by Sir Ninian Comper, better known for designing the windows of Westminster Abbey. Another connection to Westminster Abbey is the marble memorial to Sir Thomas Reeve on the south wall, sculpted by Peter Scheemakers, who produced 16 such works there.

Also of significance is the reredos behind the high altar depicting the Patriarchs of Israel, the work of Henry Woodyer. He is better known locally for building the chapel for the Convent of the Community of St John the Baptist. That sisterhood, founded in 1852 as an offshoot of this church, is still going today – it once played an essential role by providing shelter and education for the destitute women of Windsor, and their former convent can still be found on Hatch Lane, now lovingly converted into flats.

Address Clewer Court Road, Windsor SL4 5JD, www.standrewsclewer.org | Getting there
Train to Windsor & Eton Central, then a 15-minute walk, or to Windsor & Eton Riverside
and a 20-minute walk; bus 2, 8 or 703 to Windsor Boys' School | Hours Varies, but usually
Wed & Fri 10am – noon. Open Sun from 9.30am for services | Tip Down the road is The
Swan, a community-owned pub with a unique quirk: it houses its own sixth-form college,
offering hands-on teaching and work experience to students who learn better outside the
traditional education system.

78 St Leonard's Hill

Historic heights

At 295 feet high, St Leonard's Hill has always been the most fashionable hilltop in Windsor, offering commanding views of the town below. The Romans certainly had a fondness for it. One supposed Roman artefact – an ornate bronze lamp found in 1717 – caused such a stir among the *Society of Antiquaries of London* that they incorporated it as their logo. The lamp was recently re-assessed to have been of 14th-century origin, but the society is too attached to its 'Lamp of Knowledge' to sweat such an inconvenient detail.

After the Conquest, the hill came into the possession of William de Braose, but it did not remain in his family for long – William's son, also William, had a falling out with King John over unpaid arrears, which caused William to flee to Ireland. The king later built his own hermitage on the hill, which was occupied by one 'William the Hermit' and became a destination for pilgrims.

The Hermitage later gave its name to a private estate. The Duke of Gloucester built a mansion here, eventually inherited by Sir Edward Barry, son of the Portuguese copper magnate Francis Barry. Edward hated the building so much he had it blown up with dynamite – the ruins remain, and are set to be converted into a private garden, while two lamp posts at the top of the hill show where the driveway would have been.

A second manor house lives on: St Leonard's Mansion, built by James Wyatt in 1733 and later remodelled into an Art Deco villa by Horace Dodge (heir to the Dodge motor company), was a popular haunt for Joe Kennedy during his years as U.S. Ambassador. When St Leonard's Hill was later sold to private enterprise, this villa became the headquarters of first the Windsor Safari Park, then Legoland. The building has a personal significance to me: I was sent there for the telling-off of my life while working my first job as a burger-flipper in the Legoland kitchens.

Address St Leonard's Hill, Windsor SL4 4AJ | Getting there Bus 703 Greenline to St Leonard's Hill. Private road, so not accessible by car, but parking is available on nearby Wolf Lane, from where you can make your way on foot via the various public footpaths. | Tip If you see nothing else at Legoland, be sure to swing by Miniland, where the wonders of the world are reconstructed in over 40 million LEGO® bricks.

79 St Mary Magdalene, Boveney

Forgotten, but not forsaken

Poking out of a thicket of trees separating Dorney Common from the River Thames is a lonely, stoic belfry, a landmark feature dating back to the pre-Roman era. Generations of bargemen working along the river once considered this wooden tower a beacon of respite, their place of worship while working away from home.

When river traffic along the Thames dried up in the 20th century, so did footfall, and thus the church was declared redundant in 1975. It soon fell into disrepair and was even earmarked for development. Fortunately, the Friends of Friendless Churches stepped in to save it, taking out a 999-year lease and working with architect Nicola Westbury to restore the rotting tower. Today, ramblers are free to drop by during daylight hours to amble around its ancient interior.

Now frozen in time, different parts of the building tell of its impressive journey through the ages: the flint and chalk rubble walls, along with the west-facing lancet window, date back as far as the 12th century; the 15th-century pews are smothered with inscriptions, including some from Eton boys who came here to play truant; the 16th-century stained-glass window still catches the morning light just so, bathing the nave in a misty glow that makes visitors wish for the 17th-century bells to ring out once more; meanwhile, knee-shaped abrasions in the hassocks tell the stories of countless worshippers for whom this church was once the centre of their faith.

One mystery abounds: what happened to all the graves? Mr and Mrs Hall's 1859 *Book of the Thames* recounts a meeting with the warden, who remarked that the churchyard was 'thick with graves' at that time – yet even a geophysical survey by the Dorney History Group failed to find anything. The irony is almost too sad: even the dead seem to have abandoned this church.

Address Lock Path, Boveney, Windsor SL4 6QQ, www.st-mary-magdalene-boveney.org.uk | **Getting there** Roughly, a 40-minute walk from Windsor via the Thames Path; by car, B3026 to Boveney Road, then continue onto Lock Path and follow the signs for the Ramblers Car Park | **Hours** Daily, but hours vary – approximately dawn to dusk | **Tip** Follow the Thames Path east of the church to discover the quaint and quiet Boveney Lock, a great place to watch the boats going up and down the Thames.

80 _ Stag & Hounds

A pub at the centre of history

Throw a dart at a map of the old Windsor Great Forest and you're bound to hit a historic pub. Throw a bullseye, and you'll be plucking your dart out of the Stag & Hounds. The lonely tree situated on a grassy peninsula outside this picturesque country pub is known as the Centre Elm and once marked the epicentre of the forest. Tragically, the iteration you see today is a replacement. The original, which stood for some 800 years and made a popular hiding spot for poachers, was carried away by Dutch Elm Disease in the 1970s.

The Stag & Hounds started life as the headquarters of the forest's gamekeepers, later evolving into a hunting lodge and then a coaching inn. It has played a peculiar role in the royal history of England, for it was here that kings and queens would stop overnight after a hunt to soothe their saddlesore-bruised bottoms. Henry VIII and Elizabeth I are two of the building's most revered lodgers – Elizabeth was said to have made a special visit on May Days to watch the festivities from a window overlooking the green.

The property's history is still written in its rickety architecture. The oldest part of the building was a stable and, while it has been rebuilt several times since the 14th century, still retains its precariously low timber-beamed ceilings. This makes dining in the modern-day restaurant a risky activity – anyone over five feet tall should be careful not to thwack their noggins against the rafters. Still, it is worth the risk, if not to enjoy the quaint atmosphere, then certainly to partake in the sublime British-Asian fusion cuisine whipped up by chefs John Campion and Miko Mikudik. Naturally, venison appears on the menu.

If you're not in the mood for a concussion, sit yourself in the Georgian extension, where you'll find not only the bar but also a beautiful scale model of the pub built out of matchsticks by a former patron.

Address Forest Road, Binfield RG42 4HA, +44 (0)1344 483553, www.thestagandhounds.com | **Getting there** Bus 150 from Bracknell; the 151A from Wokingham also goes via Binfield Crossroads, a five-minute walk away | **Hours** Mon – Sat noon – 11pm, Sun noon – 10pm | **Tip** Just up the road is Binfield village, the childhood home of poet Alexander Pope. His legacy is recorded in the name of Pope's Meadow, where he is said to have found the inspiration for the poem 'Windsor Forest'.

81 The Stock Exchange

Buy low

Kerry Bell knew what she was doing when, in 1976, she established this second-hand clothes store in the affluent village of Sunninghill. Being a stone's throw from à la mode Ascot, where chic locals had found themselves drowning under mountains of designer bags, shoes and dresses, Bell had the idea to start a swap shop giving posh poseurs a place to buy and sell their used garms. It quickly caught on, and became Sunninghill's best-kept secret.

Almost 50 years later, the owner has changed (Jeremy Myhan stepped in after Bell's retirement in 2006), but the guiding philosophy remains the same. Debonair dressers are invited to bring their pre-loved designer glad rags for authentication and valuation and, if they are deemed to be of a high enough standard, they will be added to the hallowed rails on a Thursday morning. You'll have to be quick if you want to snap up hot stock the day it floats, especially in the weeks leading up to Ascot Week.

Choiceness plays a big part in the store's brand, and nothing less than the highest quality is accepted. Still, these luxury items can always be found at jaw-droppingly low prices. And while shoppers come for discount designer clobber from the likes of Hermès, Louis Vuitton and Prada, they stay for the feel-good factor that comes from knowing they've contributed to the circular economy. It's sustainability for the *Vogue* demographic, darling.

One person who certainly buys into the ethos is Kate Middleton, Princess of Wales, who was snapped in 2012 wearing a dress from this very store. Of course she looked fabulous, as she always does, but when the fashion mags caught wind of where she'd been shopping, a stock market bubble formed, propelling the store all the way to the front cover of *Grazia*. This was much to the chagrin of The Stock Exchange hard-cores, who suddenly found their best-kept secret had hit the mainstream.

Address 2 Queen's Road, Sunninghill SL5 9AF, +44 (0)1344 625420, www.stockexchange.org.uk | Getting there Bus 1 or 28 to High Street Shops; two hours' free parking in the adjacent Queen's Road Car Park | Hours Mon–Fri 9am–5pm, Sat 9am–4.30pm | Tip Up the road, at 56 High Street, is Chapmans of Sunninghill – not just an ironmongers, but a local institution selling everything under the sun, including a selection of local history books covering Sunninghill, Ascot and beyond.

82 Sutherland Grange
Walking among famous company

Hidden away on the outskirts of Windsor is a meadow teeming with crane's-bill and knapweed, a sanctum away from the fraught rush of the town outside. It has not one, not two, but three separate conservation areas, each overflowing with meadow-grasses, inviting bumblebees to feast on the nectar and pollen within. The slow-flowing Clewer Mill Stream runs around the north bank, where blue damselflies and water boatmen dance between the spindly branches of willow trees.

Today, Sutherland Grange is home to all of these species and many more, but they are not the most notable residents to have resided upon this Arcadian field. That honour is split between Mary Caroline Blair and Sir Dhunjibhoy Bomanji.

Let's do Mary first. In 1861, she and her husband Arthur moved into the Victorian mansion adjacent to this meadow (which retains the name Sutherland Grange) to manage the house on behalf of the Duke of Sutherland. But Mary, an infamous social climber, wanted more than a job – she wanted the Duke. And so, after Arthur died in a *verrry* suspicious shooting accident, and then the Duke's wife also passed away, she swooped. Barely four months later, she and the Duke were married, which caused such a stir that Mary was banished from high society and henceforth known as 'The Scandalous Duchess'.

Sir Dhunjibhoy Bomanji, meanwhile, was a bombastic Bombay businessman. After amassing a fortune in the world of shipping, Sir Dhunjibhoy retired to England to concentrate on philanthropic pursuits. He had a manor house at Sutherland Grange (one of three that made up his Windsor estate), which has since been knocked down, and it was here that he hosted his esteemed charity colleagues. One of those men was Field Marshal Earl Haig, who would later establish the Royal British Legion. Sir Dhunjibhoy, in turn, commemorated Haig's achievement with a statue erected at Edinburgh Castle.

Address 25 Burnetts Road, Windsor SL4 5TN | Getting there Bus 2 or W1 to Ballard Green; free parking for up to three hours on site | Tip Further up Maidenhead Road you will spot the definitive clocktower of The Willows, another of Sir Dhunjibhoy's mansion houses, and the only one still standing.

83 __ The Swans
The lesser-known members of the Royal Family

Aren't you glad you picked up the guidebook that lists 'swans' as one of the must-see things in Windsor? But hear me out, because this is the perfect place to address an age-old question: does the king *really* own all the swans in England? The answer is… kind of. He actually owns all the *unmarked* swans. Let us swan dive into the history to explain why.

We don't really know how and when the Crown first claimed ownership of the country's swans, but it must have been before the 13th century and probably had something to do with the fact that swans were a popular source of meat. Perhaps, then, the law was a form of population control, or perhaps it was to stop people nicking the king's favourite meal – either way, people didn't take to it very kindly, and by the 1230s some had taken it upon themselves to 'mark' swans to claim ownership. When this got out of hand, it led to the creation of a swan policeman known as the Royal Swan-master in 1361, then to an 'Act for Swans' in 1482/3, which stipulated who was allowed to mark, and therefore own, these birds (*quelle surprise*, it was rich landowners).

This created further headaches when it became hard to track who owned newborn swans, leading to another tradition: 'upping'. Every year, in the last week of June – a period when adult swans are in wing-moult and cygnets have not yet fledged, making them easy to catch – groups of canoes would row up the Thames with the Swan-master, picking swans out of the water and checking for marks, then marking the cygnets too. Today, two bodies continue this tradition: the Vintners Company and Worshipful Company of Dyers, who have maintained their ownership of certain swans along the Thames since the 16th century. As such, if you swing by Windsor Promenade in early summer, you may catch a glimpse of the Vintners and Dyers carrying on this curious ancient practice.

Address Windsor Promenade, Windsor SL4 1QT, www.royalswan.co.uk | Getting there
Train to Windsor & Eton Riverside, or Windsor & Eton Central and a five-minute walk;
served by most bus routes | Hours Mute swans don't tend to migrate, so they can be seen in
Windsor year round. Visit the website for dates and times of the yearly upping ceremony. |
Tip The nearby River Street toilets contain some wonderful murals depicting scenes from
Windsor's history.

84 Swinley Forest

The crucible of civilisation in the Great Forest

Easthampstead Plain was a barren heathland in the Windsor Great Forest, a popular haunt for bandits, including Dick Turpin. But when the country found itself in a timber shortage after World War I, it was planted with millions of pine trees and became Swinley Forest. Highwaymen tend to avoid this part of the world now, but in their place you will find an incredibly diverse range of animal, bird and insect species, and a treasure trove of historic artefacts that point to the ancient history of the Great Forest.

One such site is an oak leaf-shaped tract of land named Caesar's Camp (ironically, it had nothing to do with Julius nor any other Caesar). It is believed to date to around 300 B.C., and was the easternmost stronghold of a Belgic tribe known as the Atrebates. The mile-long dirt rampart around the perimeter, an august work of ancient engineering, can still be seen today – you can even hike along the precipice, if you're feeling brave.

Running past the south of this camp is a section of The Devil's Highway, a Roman road that once connected London to Silchester. The town of Wickham Bushes, which is preparing for a full excavation, developed alongside this road as a resting place for travellers – an ancient service station along an ancient M4, if you will.

The forest has long been used for military training (in fact it is still used by Royal Military Academy Sandhurst to this day). The Army trained their tank operators here during World War II, and the canyon-like tank traps they dug at that time are now popular with mountain bikers. It's also popular with directors, and has made several appearances on the silver screen: it played the role of Hogwarts Forest in *Harry Potter and the Deathly Hallows*; a misty woodland in Langvann, Norway, in James Bond's *No Time To Die*; and was recently cast as Middle Earth in Amazon's *The Lord of the Rings* serial.

Address Bracknell RG12 7QW, www.windsorgreatpark.co.uk/swinley | **Getting there** By car, follow B340 to The Look Out Discovery Centre, where parking is available | **Tip** Pack your swimming cossie and finish your day on the other side of Nine Mile Ride (one of the hunting trails established by Queen Anne) at indoor water park Coral Reef Waterworld.

85 Tally Ho Stables
Can you hack it?

'Tallo Ho!' was once a phrase walkers in the Great Park would have been familiar with, for this was the cry given by hunters once they'd spotted their quarry. It would usually be followed by the blaring of bugles and the thunderous rampaging of horses. The transformation of the Great Park from hunting ground to luscious garden means no bugles toot these days, but both the horseriding legacy and the phrase live on in this delightful stables just beyond Bishop's Gate.

From Tally Ho, visitors can partake in 'hacking' (that's equestrian lingo for 'pleasure riding'). The appeal of hacking through the Great Park is that not only is it the best way to connect with the age-old tradition of strutting down the Rides – the stretches of the park domesticated over many centuries for horses – it is the only way to get to see what lies beyond the golden, sandy paths that snake for some 20 miles around the grounds.

Riding permits are, to put it bluntly, extortionate to the have-a-go, and besides there is the small matter of getting your own steed to the starting gate. Fortunately, the guides at Tally Ho offer the full package at a very affordable rate, and with their own expertise thrown in to boot. Don't worry if it's your first time on horseback – the 37 mounts stabled here have plenty of experience carrying timid riders. On the other hand, if you're the kind of rider who feels comfortable getting up to a gallop, bear in mind the hacks tend to be slower paced. Although, if you ask nicely, the guides might let you detour through the Deer Park, where you'll have the chance to let loose.

Fun fact: Tally Ho derives its name from a farm in Winkfield where the business started in 1996. They may have moved to the other side of the Great Park, but Andrew 'Gilly' Gilbert and his team have never stopped working around the clock, such that they now offer a wide range of hacks from carriage driving to evening rides, with all equipment included – minus the bugles, of course.

Address Dell Park Farm, Bishopsgate Road, Englefield Green TW20 0XT, +44 (0)1784 479159, www.tallyhostables.co.uk | **Getting there** Set your satnav to TW20 0XU and look for the entrance via Dell Park Farm on Bishopsgate Road – the entrance is through the gate behind the farmhouse | **Hours** Tue – Sun 8am – 5.30pm, evening rides Tue – Thu from March – Sep, 6pm – dusk | **Tip** Continuing the hunting theme, The Fox & Hounds next door (www.thefoxandhoundsrestaurant.com) makes for a great place to retire after a long, hard hack.

86_ Taplow Court
Not your average Buddhist retreat

Red kites glide past the ornamental chimneys. Water trickles down the cascade in the Garden of Gratitude. Butterflies flutter through the wildflower meadows. Taplow Court is a sea of tranquillity, perched on a hilltop commanding a view so advantageous, it was once the scene of a mighty Iron Age hillfort.

Since then, the site has housed a succession of notable people. One of these was Tæppa, the Saxon warrior-prince who gave his name to this part of this world – his stunningly preserved burial mound can still be seen in the adjacent grounds. Much later, the Grenfell family moved into a French Gothic mansion built by William Burn and started their infamous debating society, 'The Souls'. Oscar Wilde, H. G. Wells and Winston Churchill were some of the eminent élites who visited in the pursuit of academic enlightenment, with socialite Ettie Grenfell as their moderator.

These days, the building hosts guests searching for a different type of enlightenment, for this time the moderator is SGI-UK, a Nichiren Buddhist organisation. SGI-UK takes full advantage of Taplow Court's scholarly atmosphere, whilst also caring for the building as if it were an ornamental garden. In doing so, they have restored the interior to its maximalist splendour, going so far as to enhance it with original art, whilst also creating their own museum featuring a reconstruction of Tæppa's burial site. They've added their own touch, too, in the form of a prayer hall, built of wood so as to achieve harmony with the environment.

Visit on one of the many open days and listen closely as you stroll about the grounds to hear a chorus of chants humming: '*Nam-myoho-renge-kyo*', a sacred vow of determination to the Buddhist way of life. The spiritual effect seems to amplify the magnitude of this already impressive house, adding a rich new flavour to its lineage. It is, truly, an enlightening experience.

Address Cliveden Road, Taplow SL6 0ER, +44 (0)1628 773163, www.sgi-uk.org/local-community/SGI-centres/taplow-court | Getting there Train to Taplow (Elizabeth Line), then a 25-minute walk | Hours Not usually open to the public, but check the website for details of upcoming open days, community events and concerts | Tip Taplow Court shares a garden fence with the equally magnificent Cliveden House, one-time scene of the Profumo Affair (arguably Britain's greatest-ever political scandal), now a National Trust site.

87 — The Temple of Augustus
The folly of empire

Here's a perfectly valid question: what the hell are the ruins of a Roman city in Libya doing in Virginia Water? The answer is long, somewhat tragic, and – given the ongoing scandal surrounding the provenance of many artefacts 'belonging' to the British Museum – probably all too familiar.

Leptis Magna was a prominent Roman city in North Africa, but when the Roman Empire fell the city was abandoned, leaving behind one of the most impressive and complete sets of ruins from all of antiquity. That was until 1816, when the British Consul General Hanmer Warrington arrived. Captivated by the ruins and inspired by the success of the Earl of Elgin, who had made a mint selling marbles from the Athenian Parthenon to the British government, Warrington decided that the ruins of Leptis Magna also belonged in England. The people of Libya didn't like this idea, of course, and took to destroying the pieces even as Warrington was loading them onto his ships – three columns that he was forced to abandon still lie on the beach.

Worse still, Warrington arrived home to find no one was interested in his ruins. They spent many years in storage at the British Museum before Jeffry Wyatville, architect to George IV, had the idea to use them to create a folly in the Great Park. The piece was finished with salvaged stone from a nearby demolished house, with the bridge running under the A329 corniced to fit the aesthetic.

Wyatt's folly was intended to reflect the historical association between the two great empires of Rome and Britain. The irony is that it does its job too well, now representing not one but two fallen superpowers. As they stand here today, weathered and moss-ridden, clearly not built for the moist climate of England, they appear not in the picturesque style Wyatville once imagined, but instead offer a bittersweet vision of the hubris of empire.

Address Virginia Water GU25 4QD | **Getting there** By car, follow A30 to Virginia Water Car Park, or A329 to Virginia Water South Car Park, then a 15-minute walk | **Tip** The ruins are one part of a trail that collectively makes up the Royal Landscape. Just round the corner you'll find the 18th-century Cascade, which takes advantage of the River Bourne's outlet from Virginia Water lake to create a truly sublime, if of course totally artificial waterfall.

88 The Thames Path

A long walk to rival The Long Walk

In the meadows around Ewen, you'll see the first faint trickles of water. Some 180 miles later, at the tremendous Thames Barrier, the River Thames approaches its fast-moving delta with the North Sea. For thousands of years, the interstitial space between these points has been the main artery pumping life-blood through the South of England. As the boats ferried to-and-fro, horses trudged along the banks, tugging the vessels through difficult stages. The ruts carved by their hooves left behind an unbroken track stretching the entire length of the river.

Despite all the wonder associated with the Thames, the idea to turn this towpath into a National Trail only gained momentum in 1977, when the Ramblers' Association – and one member in particular, artist David Sharp – created its first viable map. Even then, it took until 1996 for the Thames Path to gain the seal of approval. But it was worth the wait, for today the path is easily the best way to see Windsor (along with many other towns and cities). The ancient trackway follows the path of least resistance – never too hilly, never too muddy, and never too far from civilisation – meaning it can be tackled with nothing more than a pair of comfortable shoes.

From Egham, follow the route through Runnymede and Old Windsor, crossing Albert Bridge into Datchet. From there, it's back over Victoria Bridge and around the outskirts of Home Park to Windsor Riverside. Cross Windsor Bridge to Eton on the north bank, then walk across The Brocas and onwards to Boveney, Dorney, Bray and, eventually, Maidenhead.

Many of the places you'll find in this book can be seen via the Thames Path, but there is plenty more to discover for yourself. If you get lost, look for signs bearing an acorn, the path's symbol. Cycling is not permitted on certain stretches, but National Cycle Route 4 runs parallel, with plenty to discover there too.

Address www.nationaltrail.co.uk/thames-path | Getting there Windsor Bridge, served by both Windsor & Eton Riverside and Windsor & Eton Central Stations, makes an ideal starting point | Tip If you see nothing else along the Thames Path, make a special trip to Romney Lock for a spectacular view of both Windsor Castle and Eton College.

89 Theatre Royal
You can never have too many encores

It's not Christmas until Steven Blakeley takes to the stage in drag, alongside the cynical Basil Brush and Kevin Cruise as bumbling Chester the Jester. Year after year, classic fairy tales come to be corrupted by blue jokes and dodgy pop songs at what has become *the* Windsor Christmas tradition: the Theatre Royal pantomime.

Great actors like these have always gravitated to Windsor. One of the most renowned was Susanna Carroll, who in 1706 played Alexander the Great in *The Rival Queens* at Windsor Castle. The town's first permanent theatre was established shortly thereafter by one Mr Yates and set the standard by which dozens more would open their doors. Theatre Royal was a relative latecomer, started by Henry Thornton in an old bookshop in 1793. Its opening number was – what else? – *The Merry Wives of Windsor.*

Showtimes at Thornton's theatre strategically coincided with royal residencies at the castle, and Thornton's most enthusiastic patron became King George III, lending credence to the 'Royal' name. George's unsophisticated tastes drew him more to pantomimes than to Shakespeare, and he could often be heard roaring with laughter from the royal box when Richard Suett took to the stage as Indian caricature 'Cherub Dicky'.

After King George's death, the theatre fell on hard times. Thornton sold his failing business to Mrs Mudie, who was forced to move to new premises on Thames Street in 1815, but that building subsequently caught fire in 1908. After reopening in 1910, the theatre tried its hand at becoming a cinema, but reverted back in 1933 only to go bust eight months later. Poor ticket sales then sent the business into administration in 1996, only for a spirited local campaign to save it by the skin of its teeth.

These days, the theatre is doing solid business, but if you see any financiers approaching, you know what to shout: 'They're behind you!'

Address 32 Thames Street, Windsor SL4 1PS, +44 (0)1753 853888, www.theatreroyalwindsor.co.uk | **Getting there** Train to Windsor & Eton Riverside or Windsor & Eton Central; served by most bus routes | **Hours** See website for box office details | **Tip** Down the road from the theatre is 'antiques corner', comprising two fantastic stores with eclectic window displays: Art Deco Antiques and Wellington's Antiques.

90 Thomas Hardy Altar
No longer hidden in plain sight

It was an ordinary Sunday at All Saints' on the morning of 8 June, 2014. With the church's 150th anniversary coming up, parishioners Stuart Tunstall and Don Church thought it would be a nice idea to find the foundation stone. Don suspected it might be hidden behind the wood panelling around the altar, having noticed a gap between the fascia and the back wall. Going on this lead, Stuart lay down next to the panelling and shone his flashlight into the gap, finding what appeared to be a piece of carved stone. Little did either of them know what they had just stumbled upon.

Decades earlier, in the 1970s, the churchwardens had discovered a stack of papers stashed behind the organ. One of them seemed to be a design for an altarpiece, a masterpiece of sacred geometry annotated with calligraphic handwriting. It depicted the Lamb of God in an irradiant cruciform, flanked by the winged beasts of the Evangelists and tied together by a constellation of marble orbs, beneath three porticos of Caen stone. That would have been nice, thought the congregation, and the blueprints went ignored for 40 years.

Meanwhile, a rumour was going around that a young Thomas Hardy might have worked on the building of All Saints'. Hardy had joined Arthur Blomfield's architectural practice in 1862, around the time the firm started work on this church, and a decade before Hardy had written his famous novels. At the same time the stonework behind the altar was discovered, expert Claudius Beatty surmised that the handwriting in the blueprints was indeed Hardy's. All the pieces slotted together in 2017, when the panelling was removed to reveal Hardy's reredos – it was the first time it had been seen in 100 years.

Now fully restored, the altar adds a glorious new dimension to this Victorian church. Oh, and they did eventually find that foundation stone – it was on the outside wall behind the altar.

Address Alexandra Road, Windsor SL4 1HU, +44 (0)1753 862419, www.facebook.com/allsaintschurchwindsor | **Getting there** Train to either Windsor & Eton Central or Windsor & Eton Riverside, then a 15-minute walk; bus 8, 16, 440, 702 Greenline, 703 Greenline or W1 | **Hours** Mon–Wed & Sat 10am–4pm | **Tip** Shimmy over to the car park of the King Edward VII Hospital, where you'll find a statue of Edward himself. Sculpted by Feodora Gleichen in 1910, it was one of the first prominent royal statues to be created by a woman.

91 — The Totem Pole
Mungo Martin's magnum opus

Many a visitor to Virginia Water has stood in awe after stumbling across the Totem Pole. The stoic faces carved into this 100-foot tall, gravity-defying stretch of cedar may seem a little scary at first. But the story behind them – and the pole's creator – is as wholesome as can be.

Mungo Yanukwalas, better known as Mungo Martin, was born in 1879 to the Kwakwaka'wakw Nation of Vancouver Island. As a baby, Mungo's mother Nagayki took him to a renowned carver named Yakutglasomi with the wish that her son might also become a totem sculptor. Taking four eyelashes from Martin and using them to create a paintbrush, Yakutglasomi endowed Martin with the talent of a great artist.

The ceremony was evidently a success for, even as a young man, Martin displayed a rare talent. At a time when the heathen practice of totem carving was illegal in Canada, much of his talent went unnoticed – not that Martin minded, practising his craft mainly for his own pleasure, and to preserve the time-honoured craft of his Kwakiutl culture.

Only at the end of his life (and after the ban had been lifted) did Martin catch the attention of the government of British Columbia, who commissioned him to design a totem pole as a gift to Queen Elizabeth II to mark the 100th anniversary of the colony's founding. The Royal Pole, as it was named, bears the ancestral crests of the 10 tribes of the Kwakiutl. In June 1958, a 79-year-old Martin made the long journey to England to witness its unveiling by the Queen Mother.

The Royal Pole brought Martin great fame, but it was to be one of his last works, for Martin passed away on 16 August, 1962. He was granted a hero's funeral in Canada, comprising a festival of Kwakiutl culture and a naval procession aboard the H.M.C.S *Ottawa* to his burial site at Alert Bay. How lucky we are to have one of Martin's finest creations here with us in Windsor.

Address Englefield Green, Egham TW20 0HN | Getting there Nearby parking can be found at Virginia Water Car Park (GU25 4QF) | Hours Daily dawn to dusk | Tip Head back through the Virginia Water Lake Pavilion to enjoy a drink at The Wheatsheaf Hotel, which has had a monopoly on one of the best views of the lake since the 17th century.

92 Toy Kingdom
Who needs Legoland?

Parents, hide your credit cards. For whatever craze your child is obsessing over this month, they will surely find their panacea in Toy Kingdom. From board games to Barbie, dinosaurs to Disney, Pokémon to Harry Potter to Paddington Bear, it's all here in abundant supply, animated and electric, colourful to the nth degree. It's catnip for kids. Hamleys wishes it could be.

Toy Kingdom is one of 40 sections in Windsor's fully independent, family-owned department store *de force*, proudly a Windsor institution since 1918. Even after passing through five generations of the Daniel family, the store falls back on the same ethos established by founder Walter J. Daniel: high quality, great value, and always keeping afloat with the latest trends. It is an ethos that proved so popular with Daniel's neighbours up the road, the late Duke of Edinburgh was known to do all his Christmas shopping here. While other department stores have come and gone from Windsor over the years, Daniel has remained steadfast on Peascod Street, in a unit the family has gradually transformed from a humble cottage into a sprawling multiplex – and through it all, the beating heart has always been Toy Kingdom.

Department buyer Warren Du Preez goes to the ends of the earth to make his displays as perfect as can be: the photogenic LEGO statues are hand-built by Legoland's Master Builders; the steam train trundling around the rafters has been a mainstay since the 1950s; and there is always something new for children to interact with, from PlayDoh playdates to ride-alongs with Thomas the Tank Engine. Even the aroma hits all the right notes: rubber bouncy balls, polyester plushies, latex balloons, and the waft of acrylic face paints. It is the toy store of your own childhood nostalgia, a symphony of sensory sensations that – despite the ever-changing line-up of brands – feels forever timeless.

Address 120–125 Peascod Street, Windsor SL4 1DP +44 (0)1753 801012, www.danielstores.co.uk | Getting there Train to Windsor & Eton Central, then a five-minute walk, or to Windsor & Eton Riverside and a 10-minute walk; served by most bus routes | Hours Mon, Tue, Thu–Sat 9am–5.30pm, Wed 9.15am–5.30pm, Sun 10.30am–4.30pm | Tip Head out the back door of Toy Kingdom to see the Jubilee Spheres. Designed by 15-year-old Caroline Basra of Windsor Girls' School and unveiled by Queen Elizabeth II in 2012, the 60 stainless steel spheres represented her 60 years on the throne.

93 Trinity Yard

The cool kids' corner

It's all getting a bit Shoreditch down St Leonard's Road. Behind the gates of Trinity Yard is a small but thriving community of independent businesses. Once a stable block, then a garage, it retains – and capitalises upon – the sophisticated shabbiness of its previous tenants. It is the kind of space its landlords would call up-and-coming; the kind of space purist hipsters will pray never ups and comes at all.

Bike nerds will feel at home at The Bike Company. There are no great surprises among its range, which is testament to the team's decades of experience. Situated so far off the beaten-track, few tyre-kickers come by to waste time, leaving the staff free to offer a personalised service to every client – whether they are a hardcore rider in need of a tune up, a newbie wanting to learn the basics of bike maintenance, or a tourist looking to hire a set of wheels.

If modern interiors are more your thing, Urbansuite has been a destination for 23 years. Their collection, sourced from 40 continental suppliers, features all sorts of eclectic finds: chandeliers in avant-garde shapes hang above sofas that sit at the apex of technology and design. The chunky catalogues dotted around the store are not just for show – the team will happily acquire any of their suppliers' rarest pieces on your behalf.

Meanwhile, the avocado on toast contingent should head to Millar's Eatery. Founded in 2018 by father and son Richard and Ross, it combines their passions for food and travel. Look for the tacky fridge magnet on the wall that matches the provenance of your dish; look beyond to admire the homely decor, hand-built by Richard and Ross. Theirs, like many other indie cafés, was sucker-punched by the pandemic, but they adapted quickly and two of their additions from that time – a hole in the wall serving takeaway coffee, and a heated picnic area – have become mainstays.

Address 59 St Leonard's Road, Windsor SL4 3BX, www.thebikecompany.co.uk, www.urbansuite.co.uk, www.millarseatery.co.uk | Getting there Bus 1, W1, 2, 8, 9, 10, 16, 600, 702 or 703 | Hours Differ for each enterprise – check websites for opening and closing times | Tip Wine snobs should keep an eye out for Eton Vintners, another independent business, at 31 St Leonard's Road. Their Christmas hampers are the stuff of local legend.

94 The Two Brewers

Always brews up a good time

With its Georgian terraced mansion houses and parking spaces clogged up with supercars, Park Street feels like a tiny exclave of Mayfair. It was historically part of the road from London to Windsor, but now terminates at the public gate of The Long Walk. For anyone attempting the five-mile round trip to The Copper Horse, it is recommended to fuel up on a hearty lunch at Windsor's own last chance saloon: The Two Brewers.

There is an idiom about judging books by covers that surely applies here. For while the south-facing frontage of this pub looks bonnie and bright, with colourful hanging baskets and window planters, inside it is dark and intimate, all wood panels and dusty carpets, lit in certain parts only by candlelight and decorated not with flowers but with an eclectic gallery of old photographs and newspaper clippings. This is exactly the sort of unpretentious charm its regular punters come for, and on any given day you might find yourself drinking shoulder-to-shoulder with officers from the barracks, household staff from the Castle, or even the Duchess of Edinburgh.

Being one of Windsor's oldest public houses, the place is swimming with history, much of which remains shrouded in mystery. This is a constant source of bother to the owner, who is forever updating his signs as new information comes to light. Indeed, even the sign above the door, claiming the pub to have been established in 1792, might be wrong – it seems a licence was granted to The Two Brewers as far back as 1742, while the Grade II-listed building was built in 1709. Its original use was as an annex to a different pub next door called The Black Horse, but that establishment was shut down very suddenly in 1869 after it was discovered to be running a brothel. Given that it was operating right next to the Castle, we can only guess at the kind of clientele who might have visited…

Address 34 Park Street, Windsor SL4 1LB, +44 (0)1753 855426, www.twobrewerswindsor.co.uk | **Getting there** Train to either Windsor & Eton Central or Windsor & Eton Riverside, then a 10-minute walk from both; served by most bus routes | **Hours** Mon–Thu 11.30am–11pm, Fri & Sat 11.30am–11.30pm, Sun noon–10.30pm | **Tip** Sandwiched between the pub and Park Street Gate is the iconic Turret House, a quirky building with its own, you guessed it, turret. Don't be fooled – this is actually a folly, fulfilling roughly the same function as your or my garden wall.

95__ The Union Workhouse
From poor man's prison to million-pound homes

'Windsor is a delicious situation,' wrote Jonathan Swift in 1711, 'but the town is scoundrel.' He wasn't wrong. Windsor had become a town of two halves: on one side was the 'delicious' castle; on the other, the 'scoundrel' town, where rivers of filth flowed through the streets, vagrants festered in the rubbish heaps, and two out of every five children died before their fifteenth birthday.

The Poor Law Act of 1834 brought much-needed improvements to Windsor. Streetlamps came first, then a sewage system and gas works. Things were looking up, if you ignored the plight of the homeless – thankfully, another of Windsor's, *ahem*, improvements was The Union, a workhouse intended to take these beggars off the streets.

Despite its sublime architecture, life at The Union was nothing but hard labour. The men spent their days digging trenches to build Windsor's new roads, while the women worked non-stop in the kitchens. Still, the conditions were favourable to other workhouses of the era – the inmates were fed a good diet and received regular gifts, which may explain why drifters came to Windsor from as far afield as Ireland, Gibraltar and South Africa.

Workhouses were widely regarded as a blight on English society, and started to be shut down after World War II. In 1999, The Union was rebranded as Bear's Rails Park, a luxurious housing estate where homes now regularly go for over £1 million – truly a symbol of Windsor's transformation from scoundrel to delicious.

Still, one part of this private estate betrays its heritage as a quasi-prison. Adjacent to the back garden is 'The Spike'. Now used as a garage, this was once where men spent their days smashing stones into gravel, which was sifted out of the knee-high red hatches lining the walls. The iron bars across the tiny windows tell you all you need to know about the conditions they would have experienced inside...

Address Bear's Rails Park, 17 Crimp Hill, Old Windsor SL4 2QY | **Getting there**
Bus 8 from York House to Toby Carvery, then a 15-minute walk; by car A308 South, right
onto St Peter's Road, then right onto Crimp Hill. Private road, but parking is available at
nearby Crimp Hill Cemetery. | Tip Head back in to Old Windsor to find The Fox and
Castle off Burfield Road (www.thefoxandcastleoldwindsor.com).

96_ Upper Club
Making a Mess

Forget India vs Pakistan. The biggest rivalry in cricket stems from right here. The annual Eton vs Harrow match is such a boisterous affair, only Lord's cricket ground in London is big enough to contain it. Banterous chanting is a necessity at this match, with a particular favourite among the Harrow boys being 'No noise from the strawberry boys!' Joke as they might, these strawberries have carried Eton to 60 victories versus Harrow's 57 since the game's inception in 1805, while also putting Eton on the coveted world pudding map.

The strawberries in question are those found in 'Eton Mess', a dessert that is exceptionally easy to make – you take a handful of fruit, a chunk of meringue and whipped cream, and smash the everloving bejesus out of them. No one is sure how or when this recipe came into being, but many point to Upper Club as the birthplace. Of the several versions of the origin story, one involves an over-stimulated labrador crashing through a picnic basket and up-ending a pavlova, while another involves a boy accidentally sitting on a dessert tray. Whatever the case, we know the smashed-up recipe was around by 1893, when it was served to Queen Victoria under the slightly more appetising moniker 'Eton Mess *aux Fraises*'. It's even alleged the name was never 'Eton Mess' at all, rather just 'Mess', and has historically been made with everything from bananas to blackberries, pineapple and even gooseberries. Even the 'mess'iness of the dessert could be an anachronism – the name may have its roots in the practice of 'messing', which in Eton lingo means simply to take a meal.

Whatever the origin, there is no finer place to enjoy Eton Mess than on the touchlines of the Upper Club where, on a summer's day, you may be lucky enough to catch the Eton boys warming up for the big annual fixture against their Middlesex rivals. Just watch out for wayward labradors.

Address Slough Road, Eton SL4 6HD | **Getting there** Train to Windsor & Eton Riverside or Windsor & Eton Central, then a 20-minute walk; bus 15, 63 or 68 to Eton College, then a five-minute walk; public footpath access from Pococks Lane | **Hours** Daily dawn to dusk | **Tip** You can try Eton Mess at the hotel-restaurant that named itself after the dessert. The Eton Mess at 55 High Street, Eton, offers an Eton Mess afternoon tea, and even whips up an Eton Mess cocktail.

97 — The Valley Gardens

Garden variety

Sir Eric Savill is best remembered for the other Great Park garden that bears his name (see ch. 74), but his first addition to the Royal Landscape speaks much more to both his awesome vision, and the community spirit of gardening.

When he arrived at this site soon after World War II, Sir Eric found it overgrown with birch trees and bracken so thick the former soldiers he employed to work the land dubbed it 'Upper Burma'. In the following years, Savill would transform this space into an undulating landscape awash with rare plants from around the world. Nowhere is his achievement better represented than in the Punch Bowl, where the chasmic terrain has been expertly domesticated to offer a sublime south-facing view for the Kurume azaleas. You will find no shortage of other such aspects around the 250-acre estate. So diverse are the many species that no matter what time of year you visit, you'll always find something in bloom: bright yellow witch-hazels in winter; shocking magenta rhododendrons in spring; all the pastel shades of hydrangeas in summer; and in the autumn, the scarlet blush of maple trees along Canadian Avenue.

Perhaps the greatest achievement of The Valley Gardens was that it was built on a budget amidst the economic environment of post-war austerity. To that end, Sir Eric relied on donations from generous botanists across the country, and beyond. The aforementioned Kurume azaleas were gifted by local plantsman Jack Barr Stevenson. Plant-hunter extraordinaire Frank Kingdon-Ward contributed to the sourcing of rare rhododendrons. The acorns birthing the red oaks are believed to have been donated by the Canadian Forestry Battalion, who were stationed here during World War I.

Like any great garden, The Valley Gardens is a community effort, a testament both to Sir Eric and the many people who have (and still do) added their own contributions to this rich vista.

Address Wick Road, Englefield Green, Egham TW20 0HJ, +44 (0)1784 435544, www.windsorgreatpark.co.uk/the-valley-gardens | Getting there Valley Gardens Car Park can be accessed via the above postcode. Alternative parking can be found at Virginia Water Car Park (GU25 4QF) and Savill Garden Car Park (TW20 0UU) | Hours Daily dawn to dusk | Tip Continue your walk north to the Cumberland Obelisk, which was erected in around 1750 and dedicated to Prince William, Duke of Cumberland, who made many of his own contributions to this landscape as Ranger of Windsor Great Park.

98 The Village Shop

Puts your local off licence to shame

There you are, ambling around the Great Park, Jerusalem playing in your head as you gaze over the verdant glebes, when all of a sudden you find yourself back in civilisation. Welcome to the unimaginatively named 'The Village', the former industrial nexus of the Great Park. Founded at least as early as 1750, this settlement once produced the timber to build the Great Park's many fences. When Paul Sandby painted the scene in 1792, it was nothing more than a clearing full of diminutive shacks, but production soon upscaled and moved into the Prince Consort's Workshops.

The timber industry has since died down, but the workshops are still in use today as the Crown Estate's headquarters. Meanwhile, The Village has evolved into an idyllic garden suburb. Its Georgian cottages are rented out exclusively to Crown Estate staff – grounds-keepers and marketing managers alike are the lucky few who get to spend their lives in these model homes.

At the heart of The Village is The Windsor Great Park Post Office and General Store ('the shop', to locals). Managed by Vivien and Alan Benn, this is much more than a place for residents to collect their post: it is their café, serving sandwiches for folks to enjoy in the garden; it is their one-stop shop, selling everything from fresh bread to nappies; and it is a monument to former residents of The Village, who have left behind trinkets that tell the stories of their time here.

You too are invited to grab a cold drink and enjoy a pitstop. As you do, be sure to probe Vivien and Alan for tales from their 27 years behind the counter – they may spill some secrets about the people they've met along the way (assuming, of course, the conversation doesn't move on to their beloved Liverpool FC). Here's one: there's a rumour King George VI buried a time capsule in the wall of the shop when it was built in 1947. Oh, but I've said too much…

Address The Village, Windsor SL4 2HZ, +44 (0)1753 865471 | Getting there Only accessible on foot – nearest parking at Cranbourne Gate Car Park and Ranger's Gate Car Park, both roughly a 15-minute walk | Hours Mon–Thu 7.30am–4pm, Fri 7.30am–1pm | Tip On the other side of the nearby York Club is the Commonwealth Plantation. No one can quite remember why these trees were planted by Queen Elizabeth II, but they are dedicated to the Commonwealth countries of old, arranged in roughly the shape of a world map.

99 Welsh & Jefferies

Savile Row for schoolboys

To amble around Eton College on a school day is an absurd experience. There you will find yourself in the midst of a crowd of boys dressed as if they had walked right out of a Charles Dickens novel. But this strict and somewhat preposterous dress code is one of the many things that has established Eton College as a global brand – for this is more than a school, it is a gateway through which young men enter the upper echelons of society. Learning to dress with discipline is necessary to prepare these boys for careers in the military, as politicians and as businessmen.

Welsh & Jefferies knows this better than anyone. Based in an unassuming shop beneath the Beaks' (teachers') apartments, they have acted as the College's official tailors since 1865. For boys about to embark on an Eton education, this is one of their first stops. Indeed, the names and measurements of every schoolboy, old and new, are recorded in the shop's archives and updated with each new visit. It is the Eton equivalent of your mum marking your height on a door frame, except that in this case it establishes a life-long association between Old Etonians and their first tailor. Decades later, alumni are known to flock back to Welsh & Jefferies for their next hand-made suit.

Since 1988, the store has been run by the Kazan family, first by Elie – who fled the Lebanese Civil War to start a new life in England – and now by his son Tuffy. Even in this age of machine tailoring, the Kazans do things the old-school way: their garments are hand-cut from 100 per cent British pure wool, and finished in the workshop on-site. But they have added new flourishes too, most notably when it comes to the rather loud 'Pop' waistcoats they design for the school's Prefects. These garish vests, which symbolise the sardonic personalities of their wearers, can be seen in the gallery of photos lining the walls of the shop.

Address 13–14 High Street, Eton SL4 6AS, +44 (0)1753 853231, www.wjeton.com | Getting there Train to Windsor & Eton Riverside; bus 68 to Eton High Street; bus 15 or 63 to Eton College | Hours Mon–Fri 9am–5pm, Sat 9.30am–1pm | Tip Continue your tour of Eton tailors with a visit to New & Lingwood at 118 High Street. They are particularly renowned for producing clothing in the 'colours' of each house, sports team and society.

100 — Windsor & Eton Brewery
Knights of the pint

Windsor's history is drenched in beer. High-quality agricultural land, a robust water source and good transport links helped breweries like Jennings and the Windsor Brewery to get their hands on the necessary ingredients, and then to ship tens of thousands of barrels out of Windsor every year through the 1800s. The bubble burst in the 20th century, but the fundamentals remained, and it was only a matter of time before someone reignited the flame of Windsor's brewing heritage.

Those firestarters came in the form of Will Calvert and brothers Jim and Bob Morrison. Approaching retirement, the trio decided in 2009 to start a microbrewery as a way to keep busy. With the help of Master Brewer Paddy Johnson, they crafted a bitter named Guardsman in honour of Windsor's Coldstream Guards. The batch was a big hit, and set the team on a journey around the world in search of new ingredients, new techniques and new partners. A decade later and the founders still haven't retired, but they have re-established Windsor as a brewing hot-spot. Their unpretentious unit on Duke Street now ships a staggering 1.5 million pints per year, with a catalogue that has grown to feature everything from a craft pilsner to a dark IPA. The best way to sample everything is with a trip to the brewery itself: the one-hour tour is a whirlwind of anecdotes, a slew of samples, and concludes in the taproom, which fills up on weekends with beer lovers from around the world.

The brewery is particularly proud of its Royal Warrant, which it earned for supplying its waste yeast to feed the cattle at the Royal Farm. Around the time of a Royal ceremony, the crew will inevitably put out a new concoction in honour of their neighbours up the road. You may even spot them pulling the kegs up to the Castle on a horse-drawn cart – another in a long line of nods to Windsor's beery traditions.

Address Units 1–4 Vansittart Estate, Duke Street, Windsor SL4 1SE, +44 (0)1753 392495, www.webrew.co.uk | Getting there Train to Windsor & Eton Central, then a 10-minute walk; bus 7, 8, 71, 191, 702 or 703 to Windsor Boys' School | Hours Taproom: Mon–Sat 10am–10pm, Sun noon–8pm; brewery tours every Sat at 12.30pm & 3pm | Tip Can't make it to the taproom? You can still sample the range at The George on Eton High Street, the brewery's flagship pub.

101 Windsor Baptist Church

And then the heavens opened

Windsor is not what you'd call England's most liberal town. That's why it is such a noteworthy thing to see the LGBTQ Pride flag flying in the window of a church, of all places. But Windsor Baptist Church is not like other churches – it is a little island of social progressivism in a sea of traditionalism. Inclusivity is written into the church's charter of values, alongside community, family and creativity.

This is not just a place of worship. It is a refuge and safe space for the community. Whether they are refugees from Ukraine, victims of domestic abuse, or club-goers pouring out of nearby Atik looking for a place to keep warm while waiting for a taxi, Kat and her team of volunteers are there to support the Windsor community through thick and thin.

The church's interior is modest, but this tells a story. Once upon a time, the supersonic commercial plane known as Concorde departed from nearby Heathrow Airport, putting Windsor directly in its flight path. This caused a great calamity in 1983, when a Concorde had to turn back shortly after take-off. As it banked back around towards the runway, it pointed the thrust from its jets directly at the church below, ripping apart the already delicate ceiling of the early Victorian building and causing it to cave in on top of the organ.

The upshot of this tragedy was that, when the organ pipes were later stripped from the wall, it revealed an original Victorian feature they had been covering up – ornate gold calligraphy spelling out 'God is Love'.

Grab yourself 'the best hot chocolate in town' (claims Kat) from the Tree House Café in the foyer and take it up to the balcony, where you will find a catalogue of scrapbooks detailing this and many other significant moments in the church's history – such as the time they were forced to sell off the graveyard behind the church (don't tell the residents of 20 Russell Street).

Address Victoria Street, Windsor SL4 1EH, +44 (0)1753 868060, www.windsorbaptistchurch.org.uk | Getting there Train to either Windsor & Eton Central or Windsor & Eton Riverside, then a 10-minute walk; bus 1, 2, 16 or W1 | Hours Mon–Fri 9.30am–2.30pm, Sun 10am–12.30pm | Tip While there are plenty of board games for the kids in the church, active children will prefer the soft play gymnastics classes on offer at The Little Gym (www.windsor.thelittlegym.co.uk) over the road.

102 Windsor Cemetery

Will it put a spring in your step?

In the 1830s, a wave of hysteria swept across England. People in all parts of the country reported sightings of a terrifying apparition called 'Spring-heeled Jack', described as an eight-foot tall, gaunt man with clawed hands and glowing red eyes. No sooner had people spotted this phantom than it would bound away with great, gravity-defying leaps.

Meanwhile, in 1854, this cemetery was consecrated in Windsor's southernmost district of Spital. The first five years were uneventful – but then, as ghost hunter Brian Langston recounts, one night in February 1859 the gravedigger felt a presence. Looking up, he caught sight of Spring-heeled Jack lurking atop the cemetery gates, and went running into town to alert people. Few believed him – that was, until more local sightings started to emerge, particularly from young women who had spotted Jack lurking in their back gardens.

PC John Smith-Noble took it upon himself to investigate the cemetery. As he swept for clues, sure enough Spring-heeled Jack appeared out of nowhere. Smith-Noble tackled the creature to the ground and beat it into submission; however, on closer inspection, it was revealed to be a soldier from the local barracks, dressed in women's clothes and wielding a pistol. The PC dragged his suspect back to town, where the soldier professed his innocence, claiming he too was on the hunt for Spring-heeled Jack that night and that his disguise was merely intended to lure the beast out of hiding. The judge wasn't hearing it, and proceeded to sentence the soldier to prison on firearms offences.

Sure enough, Spring-heeled Jack never returned to Windsor Cemetery, but does his curse live on? Certainly, Spital has seen better days – nearby pubs are closing, the cemetery chapel is derelict, and, on the other side of the graveyard wall, Windsor FC are doomed to play in perhaps the ugliest kits known to man.

Address Gatehouse Close, Windsor SL4 3DB | Getting there Train to either Windsor & Eton Riverside or Windsor & Eton Central, then a 35-minute walk; bus 16, 702 or 703 to Stag Meadow; temporary parking available on St Leonard's Road | Hours Daily 8am–4.30pm, or sunset, whichever is later | Tip In all seriousness, match days at Windsor FC are a fantastic day out. The club has a lot of history, being the continuation of Windsor & Eton FC, which folded in 2011. See www.windsorfc.net for fixtures.

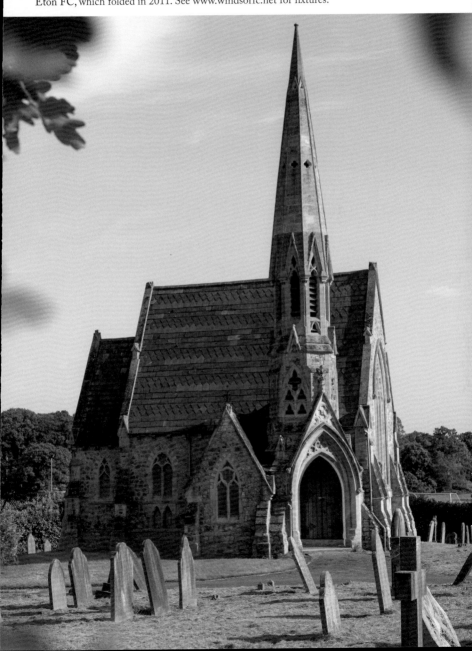

103 Windsor High Street
The final march of Elizabeth Stile

Most days around 11am, throngs of tourists jam themselves onto the pavements of Windsor High Street, clamouring for a view of the Coldstream Guards as they march from Victoria Barracks to the Castle. It's usually a joyful, festival-like atmosphere. But it wasn't always this way. Once, these crowds would have been jeering 'shame, shame!' and hurling rotten vegetables into the street. Just ask Elizabeth Stile who, in 1579, was dragged up this stretch of road by Richard Galis, landlord of The Harte & Garter. Elizabeth, along with her three friends, had been accused of witchcraft.

Richard Galis, son of the Mayor of Windsor, was a rich and powerful man with a screw loose. Local nurse Mother Dutten learned this the hard way when, while treating young Richard, he leaped up and shouted 'Witch!' That accusation spread fast, and it wasn't long before a series of calamitous coincidences unfolded, raising suspicion against Mother Dutten, Elizabeth and their two friends. When Galis' father died mysteriously, it was enough to set the whole town against the four women, and Galis fashioned himself the ringleader of a vigilante group to hunt them down. One by one, the forsaken women were marched down the High Street to the prison at Windsor Castle, before being sent to Abingdon for execution by hanging.

Today, Windsor High Street is a much more uplifting environment, a fast-flowing artery teeming with high-end shops, opulent hotels and swanky restaurants. As people make their way down this avenue, admiring the gorgeous Georgian terrace on one side and the Church of St John the Baptist on the other, it may be rather bizarre to imagine that they, along with the diners chowing down on steak, and the shoppers kitting themselves out in designer clobber, are ambling around the same space that was once the epicentre of Britain's most notorious and scandalous witch hunt.

Address High Street, Windsor SL4 1LP | Getting there Train to either Windsor & Eton Central or Windsor & Eton Riverside, then a five-minute walk; served by most bus routes | Hours The Changing of the Guard takes place on odd days at 11am – visit www.changing-guard.com for upcoming events | Tip Richard Galis' pub can still be found further down Thames Street, now a branch of The Ivy Collection.

104 The Windsor Lady

A modest statue for a modest queen

Windsor is chock full of statues of Royals, almost all portrayed in gaudy ensembles with heroic poses and ruddy faces. Queen Victoria stands by the Castle in a stiff, upright stance. King George III channels Augustus as he stares fiercely over the Great Park. The Prince Consort watches over Guards Polo Club from horseback, carried by an almost petrified posture. It is a breath of fresh air, then, to come across this statue of Queen Elizabeth II, tucked away in a quiet corner of Bachelor's Acre, the field she used to run away from the Castle to play in as a girl. For a queen whose reign was defined not by extravagance, but by humble stoicism, *The Windsor Lady* is the most honest representation anyone could ask for of Britain's longest-reigning monarch.

The work of local sculptor Lydia Karpinska, *The Windsor Lady* is remarkable for its radical understatement. It depicts Elizabeth II not in regal garb, but in a dressed-down Barbour coat, glittering headscarf, pigskin gloves and well-worn brogues. She is not in an exaggerated stance, but sits at the viewer's eye level, slightly hunched, smiling pensively, with legs crossed at the ankles. And she does not clutch the orb and sceptre, but instead cuddles Susan, her first and most beloved corgi, as five other pups roam about below. This depiction was inspired by Lydia's own brief encounter with the queen, when she had seen Elizabeth II walking her dogs past The Two Brewers pub many years before. Some classical elements feature: the queen's right index finger is raised in a nod to Leonardo da Vinci's *Lady with an Ermine*, while Susan gazes off into the distance in the style of a lion.

Unveiled in 2015, the subversive bronze work became an instant favourite with the queen. When travelling past the Castle, she would often ask the driver to stop so that she could take a moment to admire the piece.

Address Bachelor's Acre, Windsor SL4 1HE | **Getting there** Train to either Windsor & Eton Central or Windsor & Eton Riverside, then a 10-minute walk; bus 1, W1, 2, 4, 7, 8, 16, 440, 702 or 703; by car, take the B3022 to Victoria Street, nearby parking at Victoria Street Car Park | **Tip** Lydia created several model replicas of the statue, one of which can be found in the window of B. Wilkinson Jewellers at 65 Peascod Street.

105 __ The Windsor Martyrs
A sad scene from England's messy Reformation

At the junction of Thames Street and Datchet Road you'll find the George V Memorial, sculpted by Sir Edwin Lutyens. Prior to 1937, when the fountain was unveiled, this patch of earth was home to a brewery. But go even further back through history, and you'll find the site was once the scene of a malicious execution: for here, in 1543, three men became known as the Windsor Martyrs.

It all started with Robert Testwood, a devout Protestant and a singer in the Royal Chapel choir. One day, he decided he'd had enough of Catholic pilgrims coming to Windsor to visit the shrine of Good King Henry. With the winds of Protestantism blowing in his favour, he decided it was high time to teach the Catholics a lesson, and so went to the shrine and ripped the nose off the statue of the Virgin Mary. This, naturally, upset a lot of people – but it also drew many vocal supporters. Anthony Pearson, Henry Filmer and John Marbeck all joined Testwood on his soapbox, espousing their Protestant beliefs for all the town to hear.

Two men who were not particularly thrilled about this egregious display of heresy were William Simons and Dr John London, who accused the men of breaking the Six Articles, an act protecting the right to practise Catholicism in England. At a hastily put-together show trial, the prosecutors took it upon themselves to sentence three of the four men (all except Marbeck) to burn at the stake.

Two days later, a crowd of people gathered near Windsor Bridge to watch the men become martyrs. Word of this grisly execution travelled fast, and it wasn't long before Henry VIII himself heard the story. 'Poor innocents!' he exclaimed, and hurtled back to Windsor to arrest Simons and London. This merciless duo were subsequently found guilty of perjury and sentenced to an even worse punishment… They were made to ride through Windsor facing the back-sides of their horses!

Address Windsor SL4 1RQ | **Getting there** Train to Windsor & Eton Riverside or Windsor & Eton Central, then a five-minute walk; served by most bus routes | **Tip** Nearby is Castle Kebab & Grill, which remains, to this day, the best kebab I've ever had. Or, for a more traditional meal, head to The Boatman (www.boatmanwindsor.com), which since 1829 has had the enviable title of 'only pub on the river' in Windsor.

106 Windsor Railway Bridge
Brilliant Brunel's brainchild

The prototype for his Royal Albert Bridge in Saltash, Isambard Kingdom Brunel's stunning crossing over the River Thames tells the story of a fierce battle between two rival train companies and Eton College.

The first proposal for a railway connecting Windsor to the Great Western Railway at Slough was put forward by the GWR Company in 1834, but it was shot down by the headmaster of Eton College who feared a railway to London would lure his students towards the hedonism of the city. The College proceeded to scuttle a second and third proposal, and by the time the GWR came up with a fourth one a decade later, they were too late – the LSWR Company had already won approval from parliament to build their own line from Staines. But the GWR weren't about to give up. Knowing that the grounds outside Windsor Castle were in dire need of regeneration, they agreed to pay for the works, so long as they could build their own station as part of the new estate.

The Crown Commissioners agreed, but there was still the issue of Eton College. The GWR proposed a compromise: they promised the College that their line would cross the Thames in a place and in a way that would not spoil the school's bathing and rowing ponds below. But this meant the bridge would need to be suspended without piers, which created a major engineering challenge. Thankfully, Brunel had a solution. His idea was a single-span, wrought iron bridge in an 'arch and tie' style, reached by a 2,000-foot-long viaduct. In order to save time and open their line ahead of the LSWR, the GWR initially constructed this viaduct out of timber.

The GWR won the race and opened their line on 8 October, 1849. The wooden viaduct was later replaced with a brick one, while Brunel's iconic bridge over the Thames remains intact to this day – the world's oldest wrought iron railway bridge still in continuous use.

Getting there Best seen on foot from the north bank of the Thames Path; roughly a 10-minute walk from the town centre | **Tip** What better way to experience the bridge – and the lovely views it offers – than by taking a train from Windsor & Eton Central to Slough? Fun fact: the line is not electrified, and is therefore served by Class 165 and 166 diesel-powered units.

107 __ Windsor's Weird Postboxes

Royal mail

The iconic, red, cast-iron 'pillar' box has become a global symbol of Britain, with many variations in its design, from 'Lamp' and 'Pedestral', to 'Wall' varieties, and larger 'Meter' and 'Dual Aperture' types. But there are also a number of historical variations still in use, several of which can be found around Windsor.

The first is the blue 'Airmail' variety, which points to an interesting local story. On 9 September, 1911, Gustav Hamel landed his Blériot XI on the Long Walk, having flown 15 minutes from Hendon carrying a bag of letters – the first scheduled delivery by air. This caused quite a sensation, although one local newspaper at the time remarked that the practice would probably never catch on.

Nearby, by the Guildhall, is an example of a green 'Penfold' Victorian postbox. This is actually a replica made in 1988. A much darker iteration, tucked away in Windsor Royal Shopping parade, is very much an original. All postboxes were originally this shade of green, so as to make them appear unobtrusive, but this also rendered them hard for postmen to find. As such, the red postbox was declared the universal standard in 1874.

Over the river in Eton is a rare Doric Victorian postbox, notable for its vertical aperture. The Doric design was a short-lived experiment conducted at a time when no standardised model for the postbox existed. Eton was the first town to receive one of these designs – some of the other, less well-received examples were up to eight feet tall.

One more unusual postbox can be found on London Road, Sunningdale. After the 2012 Olympics, 110 postboxes across Britain were painted gold in the hometowns of Team GB's gold medalists. Sunningdale's gold postbox honours paralympian Sophie Christiansen, who scooped three golds in the Equestrian category.

Address Air Mail: corner of High Street and St Alban's Street, Windsor SL4 1PF;
Penfold 1: The Guildhall, High Street, Windsor SL4 1LR; Penfold 2: Windsor Royal
Shopping, Jubilee Arch, Windsor SL4 1PJ; Doric: outside Golden Curry, 46 High Street,
Eton SL4 6BL; Gold: outside Winkfield estate agency, Broomhall Buildings, London
Road, Sunningdale SL5 0DH | **Getting there** All Windsor and Eton postboxes are within
a 10-minute radius of both Windsor & Eton Central and Windsor & Eton Riverside
Stations; train to Sunningdale for the gold postbox | **Tip** One more noteworthy postbox to
add to your trail is the 1900s Edward VII wall box bearing the king's flamboyant insignia,
which can be found opposite the Warden's Apartment in Windsor Castle.

108 Woodside
The village built on bricks

The Industrial Revolution did not bypass Windsor Forest, as the hamlet of Woodside can testify. A look beneath the ground tells the full story. While the nearby Great Park sits on a swathe of base-rich soil, here the earth turns to sandy, acidic clay – bad for agriculture, but ideal for brickmaking. When fired, the clay from these deposits produced sublime cinnabar bricks, which were so coveted they were sought out especially for use in the Royal Albert Hall, Westminster Cathedral and Harrow School.

The bustling brick trade created many local entrepreneurs, most notably Thomas Lawrence, who at his apogee shipped 12 million bricks a year from various sites around Bracknell and Ascot. Brickmaking also transformed the landscape – the Great Forest became littered with chimneys popping out of the ground like obelisks in a necropolis, while the many clay pits dug at the time have since become ponds and lakes.

Woodside was nought but a simple outpost for the Crown's foresters until the brick industry made it a centre of local industry. The instigator was William Watson, who established Ascot Brick Works here in the late 1800s. Many hallmarks of his enterprise remain: Kiln Lane is so-named as it once boasted two mighty kilns, and the adjacent lake marks the site of his former clay pit. The majestic Woodside House is built with the area's characteristic red bricks.

The brick trade dried up in 1928, but Woodside continues to thrive. A number of great walks will lead you back to the village's two fine pubs. The Duke of Edinburgh was built on the border between the boroughs of Bracknell and Windsor, which the landlord laments makes it hard to know who collects his bins, while The Rose & Crown has capitalised on the area's trademark loamy soil to create its own vineyard – a visit is definitely recommended during the summer to try a taste of their Woodside wine.

Address Woodside Road, Windsor SL4 2DR | Getting there By car, look for signs to 'Woodside' while driving on the A332 (Windsor Road) | Hours The Duke of Edinburgh: Mon–Sat 11am–10.30pm, Sun 11am–7pm; The Rose & Crown: Mon–Thu 10am–11pm, Fri & Sat 10am–midnight, Sun 10am–10.30pm | Tip To see what the Great Forest would have once looked like in its brickmaking heyday, take a trip to Goddard Way, Bracknell (RG42 2FD), where a brick kiln chimney has been faithfully reconstructed using original Thomas Lawrence bricks.

109 _ Writ in Water

A swatch of brutalism in Runnymede

The world goes silent as you approach a strange monolith at the foot of Cooper's Hill. All that can be heard is the sludge squelching beneath your feet, for there is no lah-de-dah pathway, only a dirt trail carved by the boots of walkers who have come before you. This monument could be mistaken for a prehistoric tomb. It was measured, after all, in ancient cubits, the walls being one cubit thick, the bricks one cubit deep. But the perfect roundness of its aggregate walls is clearly modern, and don't the earthy tones make it look somewhat like the surface of Saturn?

The entrance is that of a cave – no door, only a hollow. Round the cavernous interior you walk, the tunnel growing ever darker, until, suddenly, all the light of the world bursts forth and you find yourself in the eye of God. The silence gives way to the trickling of water and raindrops splishing in the basin, where, reflecting the words inscribed in steel above it, is the 39th clause of Magna Carta: 'No free man shall be seized, imprisoned, dispossessed, outlawed, exiled or ruined in any way, nor in any way proceeded against, except by the lawful judgement of his peers and the law of the land.'

I like to think that the monument's designer Mark Wallinger's choice of words is as much a tribute to the significance of this tract of land as it is a reminder of the most important of the democratic freedoms outlined in the charter of 1215. In an age where dissidents are routinely disappeared by their own iniquitous governments, *Writ In Water* takes up an international significance.

Perhaps it is also a gentle mockery of the English system, this being a country that despite Magna Carta is without a written constitution. Our rule of government is essentially 'writ in water'. Then again, perhaps I'm overthinking it. Perhaps it is as it was intended to be – a beautiful piece of art that perfectly complements this historic landscape.

Address Windsor Road, Englefield Green TW20 0YU, www.nationaltrust.org.uk | Getting there Parking is available at Runnymede Memorials Car Park (SL4 2JL) and Runnymede Riverside Car Park (SL4 2JN), both accessed via the A308 | Tip If you're travelling from Windsor, why not go by riverboat? French Brothers ferries depart from the Promenade four times a day between April and September.

110 York Road Stadium
Where The Magpies roost

Twenty miles away from Wembley geographically, but a million miles away metaphorically, York Road can boast of one credential that sets it apart from all other stadiums, for this is the oldest continuously used football ground in the world.

York Road immediately draws associations to that overused but still perfectly succinct footballing descriptor, 'proper'. You've got proper turnstiles, a proper pie shack, proper standing terraces. Proper hand-painted murals adorn the proper concrete walls. On the pitch, nothing but proper football is played. None of that hoity-toity Premier League prancing around and falling over, no. At the time of writing, Maidenhead United play in the Conference, a proper division, where physicality is the name of the game. Proper crunching tackles, proper long balls, proper goalmouth scrambles. Time your visit for a Boxing Day home fixture and you may even get to see a proper local derby between 'The Magpies' and one of their South East rivals: Woking, Wealdstone, Aldershot. Doesn't get more proper than that.

Like any club, Maidenhead United has enjoyed and endured many ups and downs throughout its 150-year-plus history, and York Road has seen it all. From 1871, when a Mr G. Young bagged two goals against Marlow in the first ever round of the FA Cup, to 1894, when Maidenhead became a founding member of the Southern League, into the 20th century, when a constant cycle of promotions and relegations saw the club flounder in the lower leagues, with financial difficulties adding to the frustration. Things have been looking up recently and – Stop Press! – Maidenhead may soon be moving into a new, purpose-built stadium down the road. No doubt York Road will eventually become the site of (*groan*) luxury apartments, but until then, it continues to offer the kind of footballing history you won't find anywhere else. Proper.

Address York Road, Maidenhead SL6 1SF, +44 (0)1628 636314, www.pitchero.com/clubs/maidenheadunited | **Getting there** Train to Maidenhead (Elizabeth Line); served by most bus routes | **Hours** See the website for details of upcoming fixtures | **Tip** Follow the trail of supporters to The Bear (High Street, SL6 1QJ) after the final whistle. This historic pub dates back to 1485 and is often associated with the legend of the Vicar of Bray (see ch. 14).

111___Younger Bridge
If walls could talk

Perfunctorily situated beneath the abutment of the Queen Elizabeth Bridge and far enough out of town not to cause any trouble, the setting of Windsor's only significant piece of street art reveals the deep anxiety the town has with being associated with anything too 'cool'. After all, Windsor is a town whose marketing strategy revolves around the projection of an imagined, halcyon England, a land of royal pageantry and flower shows and afternoon tea. But the consequence of maintaining this façade is that the real Windsor, rough edges 'n' all, gets swept out of sight. Let's not cast our minds back to the wedding of Prince Harry and Meghan Markle, when rough sleepers were, ahem, politely escorted off the streets.

Younger Bridge, painted by artist Cosmo Sarson as part of 2012's Cultural Olympiad, is like a window into that real Windsor. Real people, with real expressions: defiant, complex, mysterious, fun. It has historical precedent, too. J. M. W. Turner was fond of painting this stretch of the Thames. His works depicted peasant women taking their livestock for a drink, boatmen bartering their wares and nudes frolicking in the water. The faces of the people who have made Windsor a living, breathing town are often lost in the marketing smokescreen, but art has always been there to immortalise them – to remind us that Windsor does in fact have a cool side.

Cosmo's mural had the honour of being the world's first piece of augmented reality street art, and was intended to help visually impaired people engage with the piece. Using an app called Aurasma, viewers could bring the faces to life and hear the students of East Berkshire College talk about their life experiences. Sadly, Aurasma has since gone to the big app store in the sky. So, unless you have a phone from the early 2010s with the app already downloaded, it's unlikely you'll experience the full effect – but perhaps the mural will speak to you nonetheless.

Address Queen Elizabeth Bridge (north side), Windsor SL4 5HU | Getting there
A 15-minute walk from town via the Thames Path. Alternatively, cross the bridge from
Windsor Leisure Centre, which is served by buses 1, 8, 702 and 703, and where you'll also
find parking. | Tip Keep your eyes peeled for a riverboat in the style of the Beatles' Yellow
Submarine, which sometimes moors close to this bridge.

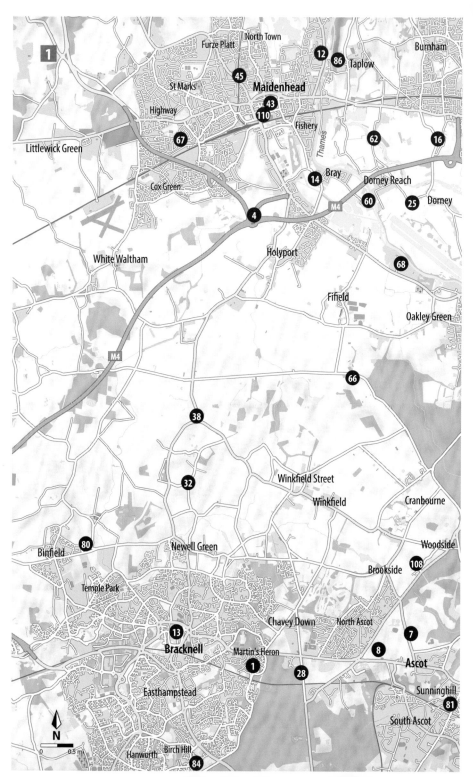

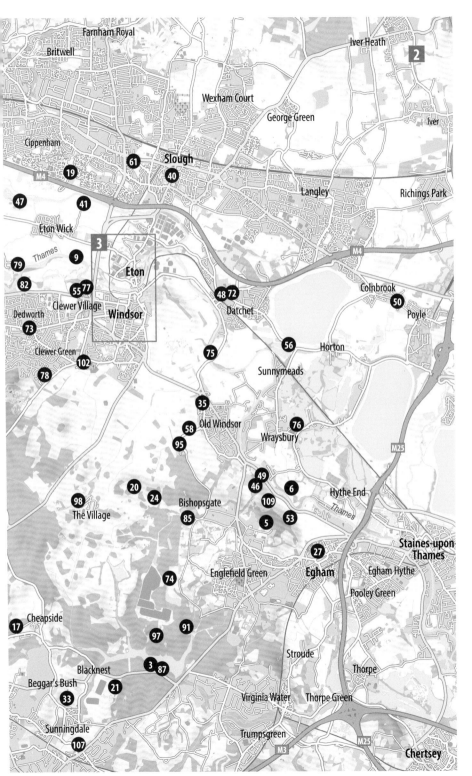

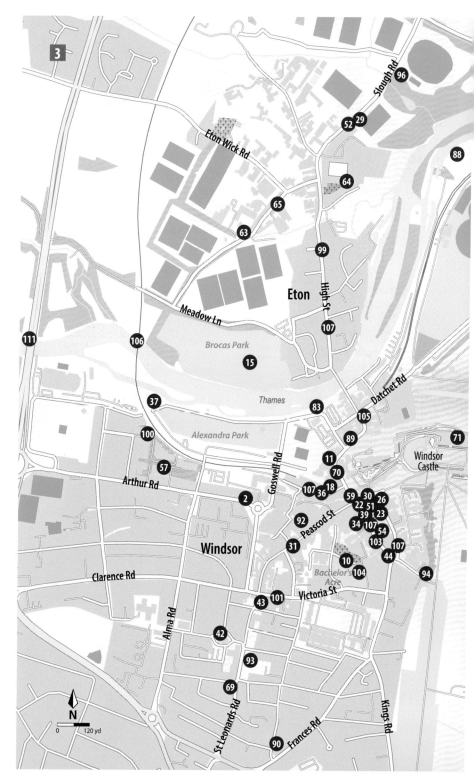

3

Slough Rd

96

52 29

88

64

65

63

99

Eton

High St

107

Meadow Ln

Brocas Park

15

Datchet Rd

111

106

Thames

105

83

37

89

100

11

Alexandra Park

71

Windsor Castle

57

70

Arthur Rd

107 36 18

2

Goswell Rd

59 30 26
22 51
39 23
34 107
54
103

92

Peascod St

31

107

44

107

10

94

104

Windsor

Bachelor's Acre

Clarence Rd

Victoria St

43 101

Alma Rd

42

93

St Leonards Rd

69

Frances Rd

90

Kings Rd

N

0   120 yd

John Sykes, Birgit Weber
**111 Places in London
That You Shouldn't Miss**
ISBN 978-3-7408-1644-5

Ed Glinert, Marc Zakian
**111 Places in London's East
End That You Shouldn't Miss**
ISBN 978-3-7408-0752-8

Solange Berchemin,
Martin Dunford, Karin Tearle
**111 Places in Greenwich
That You Shouldn't Miss**
ISBN 978-3-7408-1107-5

Terry Philpot, Karin Tearle
**111 Literary Places in London
That You Shouldn't Miss**
ISBN 978-3-7408-1954-5

Emma Rose Barber,
Benedict Flett
**111 Churches in London
That You Shouldn't Miss**
ISBN 978-3-7408-0901-0

Laura Richards, Jamie Newson
**111 London Pubs and Bars
That You Shouldn't Miss**
ISBN 978-3-7408-0893-8

Nicola Perry, Daniel Reiter
**33 Walks in London
That You Shouldn't Miss**
ISBN 978-3-7408-1955-2

Ed Glinert, David Taylor
**111 Places in Oxford
That You Shouldn't Miss**
ISBN 978-3-7408-1990-3

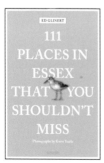

Ed Glinert, Karin Tearle
**111 Places in Essex
That You Shouldn't Miss**
ISBN 978-3-7408-1593-6

Ed Glinert, David Taylor
**111 Places in Yorkshire
That You Shouldn't Miss**
ISBN 978-3-7408-1167-9

David Taylor
**111 Places in Newcastle
That You Shouldn't Miss**
ISBN 978-3-7408-1043-6

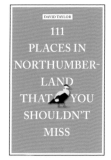

David Taylor
**111 Places in Northumberland
That You Shouldn't Miss**
ISBN 978-3-7408-1792-3

David Taylor
**111 Places along Hadrian's Wall
That You Shouldn't Miss**
ISBN 978-3-7408-1425-0

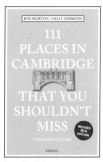

Rosalind Horton,
Sally Simmons, Guy Snape
**111 Places in Cambridge
That You Shouldn't Miss**
ISBN 978-3-7408-1285-0

Phil Lee, Rachel Ghent
**111 Places in Nottingham
That You Shouldn't Miss**
ISBN 978-3-7408-1814-2

Ben Waddington, Janet Hart
**111 Places in Birmingham
That You Shouldn't Miss**
ISBN 978-3-7408-1350-5

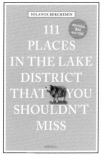

Solange Berchemin
**111 Places in the Lake District
That You Shouldn't Miss**
ISBN 978-3-7408-1861-6

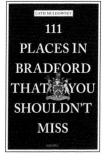

Cath Muldowney
**111 Places in Bradford
That You Shouldn't Miss**
ISBN 978-3-7408-1427-4

Kim Revill, Alesh Compton
111 Places in Leeds
That You Shouldn't Miss
ISBN 978-3-7408-2059-6

Michael Glover,
Richard Anderson
111 Places in Sheffield
That You Shouldn't Miss
ISBN 978-3-7408-1728-2

Elizabeth Atkin, Laura Atkin
111 Places in County Durham
That You Shouldn't Miss
ISBN 978-3-7408-1426-7

Lindsay Sutton, David Taylor
111 Places in Lancaster
and Morecambe That
You Shouldn't Miss
ISBN 978-3-7408-1996-5

Julian Treuherz,
Peter de Figueiredo
111 Places in Manchester
That You Shouldn't Miss
ISBN 978-3-7408- 1862-3

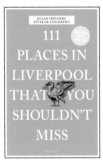

Julian Treuherz,
Peter de Figueiredo
111 Places in Liverpool
That You Shouldn't Miss
ISBN 978-3-7408-1607-0

Katherine Bebo, Oliver Smith
111 Places in Poole
That You Shouldn't Miss
ISBN 978-3-7408-0598-2

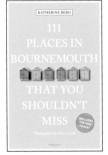

Katherine Bebo, Oliver Smith
111 Places in Bournemouth
That You Shouldn't Miss
ISBN 978-3-7408-1166-2

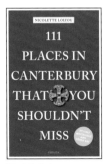

Nicolette Loizou
111 Places in Canterbury
That You Shouldn't Miss
ISBN 978-3-7408-0899-0

Rob Ganley, Ian Williams
111 Places in Coventry
That You Shouldn't Miss
ISBN 978-3-7408-1044-3

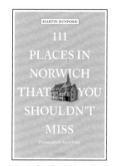

Martin Dunford, Karin Tearle
111 Places in Norwich
That You Shouldn't Miss
ISBN 978-3-7408-1733-6

Martin Booth, Barbara Evripidou
111 Places in Bristol
That You Shouldn't Miss
ISBN 978-3-7408-2001-5

Martin Booth, Barbara Evripidou
111 Places for Kids in Bristol
That You Shouldn't Miss
ISBN 978-3-7408-1665-0

Alexandra Loske
111 Places in Brighton
and Lewes That You
Shouldn't Miss
ISBN 978-3-7408-1727-5

Justin Postlethwaite
111 Places in Bath
That You Shouldn't Miss
ISBN 978-3-7408-0146-5

Gillian Tait
111 Places in Edinburgh
That You Shouldn't Miss
ISBN 978-3-7408-1476-2

Tom Shields, Gillian Tait
111 Places in Glasgow
That You Shouldn't Miss
ISBN 978-3-7408-1863-0

Gillian Tait
111 Places in Fife
That You Shouldn't Miss
ISBN 978-3-7408-1740-4

From Jonjo, with thanks to mum and dad, Scarlett, and everyone from the Bracknell Writers Group for all your support. From James, to Louise, Kate and Steph with all my love. And from both of us, to the 111 people (at least) we have met in the course of writing this book, for all your hospitality, kind words and for the incredible stories you've given us.

Jonjo Maudsley is a writer, editor and historian from Bracknell, Berkshire. By day, he manages copywriting agency Scon, by night he runs the Bracknell Writers Group, and on lucky occasions he gets to pen travel stories for the likes of *The Mirror* and the *Independent*. His secret passion is the study of urban history, a subject he took all the way to Master's level.

James Riley is an accomplished photographer and videographer originally from Berkshire. A graduate of Solent University's renowned TV and Video Production course and founder of Ellipsis Creative, a highly sought-after creative agency in London, James's portfolio has taken him worldwide, showcasing his skills in capturing captivating moments across diverse genres.

The information in this book was accurate at the time of publication, but it can change at any time. Please confirm the details for the places you're planning to visit before you head out on your adventures.